Price Fulton, Frank D. Smaw Jr.

Wilmington directory

Including a general and city business directory for 1865-66

Price Fulton, Frank D. Smaw Jr.

Wilmington directory

Including a general and city business directory for 1865-66

ISBN/EAN: 9783337711702

Printed in Europe, USA, Canada, Australia, Japan

Cover: Foto ©ninafisch / pixelio.de

More available books at **www.hansebooks.com**

WILMINGTON DIRECTORY,

INCLUDING A

General and City Business

DIRECTORY,

FOR

COMPILED BY

FRANK. D. SMAW. JR.

WILMINGTON, N. C.:

PUBLISHED BY P. HEINSBERGER,
BOOK-BINDER AND BLANK BOOK MANUFACTURER,
JOURNAL BUILDINGS.

FULTON & PRICE, STEAM POWER PRESS PRINTERS:
1865.

HISTORICAL SKETCH OF WILMINGTON, N. C.:

BY C.

NEW HANOVER COUNTY was formed in 1728, and called, in honor of the House of Hanover, then on the English throne.

WILMINGTON, its capital, the most populous and commercial town in North Carolina, named in compliment of Spence Compton, Earl of Wilmington, is situated upon the East bank of Cape Fear, or Clarendon river in North latitude 34 deg. 12 min., (48), longitude 77 deg 56 min. (18) West

It is below the confluence of the North East and North West branches The first runs up into the interior, in the direction of Duplin, and the latter past the town of Fayetteville, one hundred and twenty miles, to Haywood, in Chatham county, where it first assumes the name of CAPE FEAR, being formed by the junction of the Haw and Deep Rivers.

Like many other places, its fortunes have been fluctuating and its progress slow. The first settlements were made about one hundred and thirty-four years ago, and originally called Newtown, then New Liverpool, and finally WILMINGTON.

France having declared war against England in 1744, a fort was ordered to be built by the Legislature of North Carolina, to mount twenty-four pieces of cannon, on the sea coast, which was accordingly erected at what is now known as the village of Smithville, and called Johnson, in honor of Gov. Gabriel Johnson.

Upon the death of Governor Johnson, Rice succeeded to his authority, and upon his death in a very short time, Matthew Rowan, the senior counsellor, was qualified in his stead, in Wilmington, on 1st February, 1754.

About this time, Rowan received an express from Gov. Dinwiddie, of Virginia, informing him of the alarming movements of the French on the Ohio, and that GEO. WASHINGTON had been sent there to examine and report, &c., and that he desired assistance from North Carolina.

Rowan, accordingly, issued his proclamation for the Legislature to meet in Wilmington, on the 19th of February, 1754, which met accordingly, and appropriated one thousand pounds for raising and paying such troops as might be sent to Virginia.

Col. JAMES INNES, of New Hanover, marched at the head of a detachment, but no preparation having been made by Virginia for supplies and quartermaster's stores, Col. Innes returned to North Carolina.

A London Magazine of 1761 reports that a storm occurred, in North Carolina, which began on Monday, the 20th of September, and continued until Friday, but raged with most violence on the 23d. Many houses were thrown down, and all the vessels, except one, in Cape Fear river, driven ashore It forced open a new channel at a place called the Haul-Over, between the Cedar House and Bald Head. This new channel was found on soundings to be eighteen feet at high water, and is near half a mile wide.

In the town of Wilmington, in 1765, on the 3d of April, Wm. Tryon qualified as Commander-in-Chief and Captain-General of the Province of North Carolina. Bred a soldier, and not destitute of mind, he was disposed to rule with an iron hand, and acquired in consequence of his despotic sway the *soubriquet* of the "Great Wolf of North Carolina." He would wheedle or cajole, whenever his interests were advanced by such conduct, or adopt an opposite policy when it conduced to his interests. He first met the General Assembly in the town of Wilmington, on 3d of May, 1765, one hundred years ago. During this session, the Assembly was so much exercised on the subject of the Stamp Act, that Tryon prorogued it, upon the 18th May of the same year.

The Speaker of the House, John Ashe, told Gov. Tryon this act would be resisted to the death. Accordingly, upon the arrival of the Diligence sloop-of-war, in the Cape Fear river, Ashe, of New Hanover, and Col. Waddell, of Brunswick, marched at the head of the men of these counties to Brunswick, before which town the ship lay, prevented the Captain from landing the stamped paper; seized the sloop-of-war's boat, placed it on a cart, flew a flag from the mast-head and marched in triumph to Wilmington, where, at night, the town was illuminated. The next day they called upon the Governor and demanded that he would desist from any attempt to execute the Stamp Act, and to surrender to them James Houston, the Stamp Master, an inmate of Tryon's house. He at first refused, but ultimately yielded to the popular demand. In case of refusal, they threatened to burn the Palace and its inmates. Whereupon Houston was reluctantly surrendered to the popular demand, and then taken by them to the Market House, and there forced to take an oath not to execute the duties of Stamp Master. These acts were performed in open day, by well known persons, and yet they are "not of the few, the immortal names, that were not born to die."

"These are deeds which should not pass away,
And names that must not wither."

In July, 1774, on the Boston Port Bill being enacted by Parliament, the citizens of Wilmington met and declared : "the cause of Boston is the common cause of America," and Parker Quince was sent with a ship load of provisions to succour the Bostonians.

On the 23d November, 1774, the citizens of Wilmington elected a Committee of Safety, of which CORNELIUS HARNETT, JOHN QUINCE, FRANCIS CLAYTON, WM HOOPER, ROBERT HOWE, JOHN ANCRUM, ARCH. McLAINE, JOHN ROBERTSON and JOHN WALKER were members.

When Gov. Martin, the last of the royal Governors and Tryon's successor, summoned His Majesty's Council to attend him, on board the sloop-of-war in Cape Fear river, January, 1776, the Committee informed the members, then on their way, they could not, consistent "*with the safety of the country, permit them to attend the Governor.*"

Upon the 27th of February, 1776, the battle of Moore's Creek was fought, between the Scotch Tories, under Brigadier General McDonald, and the Whigs, under Lillington and Caswell, in which the Tories were badly defeated, with the loss of their military chest. This victory entirely thwarted the plan of Gov. Martin, which was to form a junction with Sir Peter Parker, and Maj. Gen. Sir H. Clinton, and thus to overrun the Southern country. Delayed by weather, the military and naval armament did not arrive in the Cape Fear until the 18th of April, 1776. The whole naval force consisted of thirty-six ships.

While here Gen. Clinton ravaged Kendall, the seat of General ROB'T HOWE. History avers that he and Cornwallis surrounded the dwelling, and after murdering three women, they marched to Orton, where military stores and provisions were deposited, but information of their purpose having preceded them, they had been removed, and the buildings alone were sacrificed. The fleet sailed from the Cape Fear on the 1st June, and arrived off Charleston on the 4th. In a proclamation of free pardon "to all such as shall lay down their arms and submit to the laws," given on board the Pallas transport, by Sir Henry Clinton, on the 5th of May, 1776, CORNELIUS HARNETT and ROBERT HOWE were excluded from its benefits.

The following flattering sketch of the manners and customs upon the Cape Fear, at the period of which we are speaking, is from the pen of Mr. A. M. Hooper, contained in his biography of his distinguished kinsman, the Hon. Wm. Hooper, one of the signers of the Declaration of Independence in 1776. The Hoopers have always been a family of scholars:—

"Hospitality carried to the extreme, and excessive fondness for conviviality, were the characteristics of those days. In fact, every class of society became infected by the example; and numbers of old families, now reduced to comparative poverty, have reason to rue the prodigal liberality of their ancestors."

The British Governor Martin, having occasion to reply to an address of the inhabitants of Wilmington, presented by Mr. Hooper, styled it *"the region of politeness and hospitality."*

Festive entertainments, balls, every species of amusement which song and dance could afford, were indulged in. Everywhere, on the river Cape Fear, were men of fortune, related by blood, or connected by marriage.

This general ease and prosperity was highly favorable to the cultivation of polite letters and to the development of talents of a certain kind. The state of manners tended to awaken a spirit of improvement, which pervaded the whole community. Every family possessed a collection of the best English authors, besides which there was a public library, supported by a society of gentlemen, and styled "The Cape Fear Library." Wit and humor, music and poetry, were drawn into action in social and convivial intercourse. Conversation was cultivated to a high degree. Emanating from letters or science, or growing out of the busy scenes of life, it always teemed with instruction and imparted delight. The point of honor was understood and recognized, and the slightest approach to indignity resented. In this exercise of colloquial talent, the ladies participated and heightened the pleasures. Then they were not, as now, as early instructed, or perhaps, not instructed at all, in the rudiments of knowledge; but they derived from reading, and imbibed from an association with eminent persons of the opposite sex, a tincture of taste and elegance, and they had a softness, sentiment, grace, intelligence—every quality which in the female sex can inspire and exalt the enthusiasm of romantic passion.

In the hospitable conviviality of those times, allurements to dissipation were greater than social life usually presents. The actors were far above the cast of ordinary *bon vivants*. Among those were Dr. Eustace, the correspondent of Sterne, who united wit and genius, and learning and science; HARNETT, who could boast a genius for music, and taste for letters; Lloyd, gifted with talents and adorned with classical literature; Pennington—(comptroller of the port, and afterwards Master of Ceremonies at Bath, England)—an elegant writer, admired for his wit and his highly polished urbanity; McLaine, whose criticisms on Shakspeare would, if they were published, give him fame and rank in the republic of letters; Boyd, who, without pretensions to wit or humor, possessed the rare art of telling a story with spirit and grace, and whose elegiac numbers afforded a striking contrast to the vivid brilliancy of the scenes in which he figured; Judge Maurice Moore, endowed with versatile talents, and possessed of extensive information—as a wit, always prompt in reply, as an orator always "daring the mercy of chance;" Howe, whose imagination fascinated, whose repartee overpowered, and whose conversation was enlivened by strains of exquisite raillery. Wit and humor, and music and poetry, displayed all their charms among the festive deities, and heightened the glow of delight. Is it to be wondered at, that the banquet was often carried to an "injurious excess?" Mr. Hooper played his part among these distinguished wits, and shed a classic lustre over these refined revels.

Blended with the history of the Cape Fear, at this period, is that of FLORA McDONALD, the fair and gentle protectress of the fugitive Charles Edward.

Encouraged by the representations of their countrymen, who had removed to the Cape Fear, McDonald of Kingsburg, and his wife Flora, arrived upon its banks in about 1775 or 1776. At the battle of Moore's Creek, he having joined the royal standard, was taken prisoner and confined in Halifax jail. Being finally released, he and Flora returned to Scotland. On the passage out, they became engaged with a French man-of-war. Flora remained on deck during the action, encouraging the men by her presence and counsel. The enemy was beaten, but during the confusion of the fight Flora was thrown down and had an arm broken. She is said to have remarked: "I have hazarded my life for the house of Stuart and for the house of Hanover, and I do not see that I am a great gainer by either."

Dr. Samuel Johnson, who had been her guest, says: "She is a little woman, of a genteel appearance, and uncommonly mild and well-bred." She died March 4th, 1790, and was buried in a shroud made of the sheets in which Charles Edward had slept at Kingsburg.

MEMBERS OF THE HOUSE OF COMMONS,

From the Borough of Wilmington, from 1774 to 1836, when the Borough representation was abolished by the Convention of 1835.

1774, Francis Clayton.
1775, Cornelius Harnett.
1776 to 1784, Wm Hooper.
1783 to 1786, Arch McLaine.
1787, Josh Potts.
1788 to 1791, Edward Jones.
1792 to 1809, Josh G Wright.
1810 to 1815, Wm W Jones.
1816 and 1817, Ed B Dudley.
1818 Wm B Meares.
1819 to 1822, J D Jones.
1823 Mont W Campbell.
1824 and 1825, Rob't H Cowan.
1826 and 1827, Jos Alston Hill.
1828 John Walker.
1829 and 1830, Jos A Hill.
1831 and 1832, Dan'l Sherwood.
1833 J D Jones.
1834, Ed B Dudley.

Contemplating this array of representative men, we are struck by the combination of wit, humor, highly cultivated genius, and refined culture with tact, talent, political sagacity and comprehensive statesmanship.

Any constituency might be justly proud of such representatives, and should be careful to remember as their interests and fame suffered no detriment while under their guardianship, their memories should be kept ever fresh in the minds of the people. As something is due in life to death, so something is due from the living to the dead.

We are told by Diodorus Siculus that the ancient Romans were in the habit of placing in the vestibules of their houses busts of the illustrious dead, so that, in passing in and out, their virtues and their example might become familiar to their youth, thus early accustoming them to the contemplation of greatness and insensibly implanting a desire to achieve it Let us profit by the suggestion.

Among other sons, who have conferred honor upon our town, are Johnson Blakely, Col. Wm. McRee, Col. Wm. Gibbs McNeil, Col. Sam. McRee, Capt. Alex. J. Swift, Capt. J. H. K. Burgwin, and Lieut. Wm. H. Wright, all of whom, except Blakely, wore *eleves* of West Point.

Col. Wm. McRee is generally represented, by the army, as having been the ablest and most profoundly accomplished soldier in all that pertains to his profession, who has ever belonged to the United States army. He is said to be the father of the corps of engineers, and served in the capacity of chief of that corps, upon the Northern frontier, during the war of 1812, upon the staff of Gen. Jacob Brown. At the close of the war, it was proposed by J. C. Calhoun, on account of his pre-eminent abilities, to place him at the head of that department, but he declined the preferment because it would overslaugh a brother soldier, Gen. Armistead, and his sense of professional etiquette would not allow him to be a party to such an act of injustice. He shortly after resigned, in consequence, it is understood, of the Government conferring equal rank in his corps upon the French Gen. Bernard, who had recently arrived on this continent and entered our service. McRee afterwards became engineer in-chief of the State of Missouri, and died of cholera, in St. Louis in 1831.

Gen. Wm. Gibbs McNeil belonged to the topographical corps, and was for a long while, before he left the army, engaged in civil service, in the State of Maryland, upon the Baltimore and Ohio Railroad, and afterwards in Massachusetts. After he left the service, he became the chief engineer of the Charleston and Cincinnati Railroad. He possessed in an eminent degree what is known in the military profession as the *coup d'œil*.

Swift and Burgwin were both martyrs to the war with Mexico. The former dying in New Orleans of disease contracted at Vera Cruz, and the latter fell a victim at Puebla de Taos, in obeying a senseless order to charge a stone church. Being assured in his expiring moments that justice should be done his memory, his dying utterance was, "*that justice should be done to his men.*" Wm. Henry Wright, an accomplished officer and soldier, was never in active service. The greater part of his life, after leaving West Point, was spent in the construction of FORT WARREN, located in the harbor of Boston, Massachusetts. His chief reputation, however, is based upon the publication of his work on mortars.

JOHNSON BLAKELY emigrated with his father from Ireland, and arrived in Wilmington in 1783–'84, aged about three years. It was not long before the father died, and Johnson became the *protege* of Col. Edward Jones, who charged himself with the nurture and education of young Blakely, a duty which he faithfully discharged. In the fulness of time he was sent to the University, and soon after the completion of his course there, joined the United States Navy as Midshipman, and in 1800 he was ordered to the Mediterranean with Com. Preble, and soon, by attention to duty, and the propriety of his conduct, secured the confidence and regard of his commander, his officers and his men. Meeting with speedy promotion, he was ordered to the Wasp, and sailed from Portsmouth, N. H.

In June, 1814, he fell in, off the English coast, with His Majesty's sloop-of-war Reindeer, Capt. Manners. A sharp action ensued. Manners, the first lieutenant, and many of the crew were killed and the ship surrendered. Blakely writes the Department: "We fell in with, engaged, and after an action of nineteen minutes, captured His Britanic Majesty's sloop-of-war Reindeer, Capt. Wm. Manners, commander." From the first to the fifteenth of August, he captured fifteen of the enemy's ships. In one of these he placed Lieut. Geisenger, as prize master, with dispatches for the Government. Geisenger arrived safe in Savannah, 4th November, 1814, and brought the last authentic intelligence ever received of the gallant dead. Capt. Blakely married in 1813 Jane Hooper, and left an only daughter, Udney.

In December, 1816, the Legislature of North Carolina resolved unanimously, that the child should be educated at the expense of the State, which was accordingly done. She acquired her education in Philadelphia, and shortly after married, and went to reside in the West Indies. Before leaving this country, however, she sent her portrait, as a token of kind remembrance, to the family of her father's early patron.

We have already learned that Wilmington entitled herself to a just renown in her struggles anterior to, pending, and succeeding to the revolution of 1776, during the wars of 1812 and also that with Mexico. How shall we characterize her conduct in the bloody drama which has been enacting from 1861 to 1865, and which may with truth be styled "the bloodiest picture in the book of time ?" Let the blood of her sons which has soaked every battle field from Fisher to Sharpsburg, and whose bones are bleaching from Charleston to Gettysburg answer.

The number of men contributed could be easily computed, but the value of their services could not be so readily ascertained. The amount of munitions of war, quartermaster's and commissary's stores, and other advantages secured by the exports and imports of the blockade running, it is alike difficult to estimate. They exceed many millions!

In 1819 a great fire occurred, which consumed about two hundred buildings, and property valued at $1,000,000. Population in 1830, about 3,000; 1840, 4,744; 1850, 7,264, 1853, about 10,000; in 1865, about 15,000.

COMMERCIAL STATISTICS.

Shipping of the district, June 30, 1854, according to Custom House returns, amounted to an aggregate of 10,684 tons registered, and 9,271 tons enrolled and licensed. The foreign and coastwise arrivals in 1852, exclusive of Charleston steamers and North Carolina coasters, were 753.

The following is the table of principal articles exported, coastwise and foreign, in 1853-'54:

	1853.		1854.	
	Coastwise.	Foreign.	Coastwise.	Foreign.
Spirits Turpentine, bbls.,	113,717	1,457	119,308	1,314
Crude " "	51,828	21,454	65,102	
Rosin, "	369,770	10,679	441,692	12,071
Tar, "	21,609	4,521	32,919	11,603
Pitch, "	5,019	1,904	4,624	7,188
Flour, "	1,349	86	14,431	1,001
Timber, feet.	1,030,441	85,154	1,350,263	630
Lumber, "	25,646,792	12,511,158	20,003,958	206,915
Shingles,		5,223,750		11,118,180
Staves,		154,783		5,128,259
Ground Peas, bushels,	69,624	87	91,807	133,819
Cotton, bales,	7,515		10,328	32
" Sheeting, bales,	2,320		1,689	
" Yarn, "	2,581		1,573	
" Waste, "	317		206	
" Warp, "	122		181	
Paper, News, bundles,	2,120		2,805	
Wool, bales,	182		39	
Rice, clean, casks,	1,724	252½	401	164
" rough, bushels,	102,917		137,672	

COMPARATIVE TABLE

Of Exports from the Port of Wilmington, N. C., compiled from the reports of the DAILY JOURNAL, for the first quarter of 1861, compared with the first quarter of 1860, ending 31st March of each year.

	1860		1861	
	Coastwise.	Foreign.	Coastwise.	Foreign.
Spirits Turpentine, bbls.,	27,133	3,836	20,643	728
Crude " "	21,100	3,577	11,987	2,020
Rosin, " "	104,403	13,356	75,754	11,939
Tar, " "	17,994	1,238	22,597	2,593
Pitch, " "	1,838	514	1,090	185
Timber, Pitch Pine, feet,				65,000
Lumber " "	980,317	2,803,750	1,555,608	3,687,131
Shingles,	14,000	514,500		1,859,000
Staves,			5,545	
Pea Nuts, bushels	57,071		65,138	
Flour, bbls.,	250	10		
Cotton, bales,	10,791		22,724	713
" Sheeting, bales,	279		449	
" Yarn, "	430		239	
" Waste, "				
" Warp, "				
Rice, rough, bushels.	55,670		36,169	
Rice, clean, casks,	1	5	30	
Paper, News, bundles,	509			
Wool, bales,	1		20	
Wheat, bushels,	236			

MISCELLANEOUS—COASTWISE.

Flaxseed, 510 bushels; Empty Barrels, 73; do. Kegs, 406; do. Hhds., 7; Soap Stone, 379 bbls.; Liquor, 52 bbls.: Merchandise, 226 packages; Dried Fruit, 10 boxes, 1,246 bags, 449 bbls.: Hides, 500; Fish, 5 bbls.; Old Iron 105 tons; Corn, bushels, 19,138; Tobacco, 9 boxes; Bones, 18 bags; Sugar, 3 hhds.; Copper Ore, 282 bbls.; Old Copper, 5 bbls.; Potatoes, 5 bbls.; Soap, 37 boxes; Juniper, 86 cords; Beeswax, 1 bag, 20 bbls.; Oils, 30 bbls.; Rags, 30 bales; Tallow, 8 bbls.; Salts, 25 sacks; Eggs, 4 boxes, 8 bbls.; Fur, 10 boxes, 3 bags, 10 bbls., 13 hhds.; Molasses, 76 hhds.; Hay, 61 bales.

FOREIGN.

Corn, bushels, 200; Peanuts, 40 bushels; Peas 94 bushels.

We publish to-day our table of exports from the port of Wilmington, for the quarter ending March 31, 1861, as compared with those for the corresponding period of 1860. In Spirits Turpentine there is a falling off, as there is in every article of naval stores, with the single exception of Tar, which shows a slight increase.

In Timber, Lumber, Shingles and Staves, there is an increase, especially in the foreign shipment. There is a slight gain in Peanuts, and a decided loss in Rough Rice, but the most marked feature is in the increase in Cotton from 10,791 to 22,724 bales coastwise, 713 foreign, this increase far more than making up for any falling off in naval stores. Owing to the short Wheat crop last year in our Middle and Western counties, there has been no shipments of breadstuffs from our port, and little of North Carolina produce from *any* port.

F. L. BAUER,
M. M. KATZ,

No. 23 Market Street,
WILMINGTON, N. C.,

WHOLESALE AND RETAIL DEALERS IN

STAPLE AND FANCY
DRY GOODS,
SILKS, MERINOS,
ALPACAS,
FRENCH MILLINERY,
EMBROIDERIES, NOTIONS,
BALMORAL AND HOOP SKIRTS,
DOUBLE ELLIPTIC SKIRTS,
White Goods of every variety,
MOURNING AND FANCY VEILS,
HATS AND CAPS,
CLOTHING,
BOOTS AND SHOES, AND FURNISHING GOODS.

CALL AND PRICE, AND YOU ARE SURE TO GET SUITED.

BROWN & ANDERSON,

IMPORTERS AND DEALERS IN

FINE WATCHES, CLOCKS, JEWELRY, SILVER WARE, TABLE AND POCKET CUTLERY,

Pistols, Fancy Articles, &c.

Concave and Convex Spectacles, to suit all ages.

WATCHES AND JEWELRY

REPAIRED WITH NEATNESS AND DISPATCH.

No. 37 Market Street, (Old Stand,)

WILMINGTON, N. C.

G. R. FRENCH & SON,

WHOLESALE AND RETAIL DEALERS IN

BOOTS, SHOES AND LEATHER,

AND A GENERAL ASSORTMENT OF

SHOE STOCK,

NO. 11 MARKET STREET,

WILMINGTON, N. C.

A. WEILL. G. ROSENTHAL.

A. WEILL & CO.,

WHOLESALE AND RETAIL DEALERS IN

FOREIGN AND DOMESTIC DRY GOODS,

CLOTHING,
GENT'S FURNISHING GOODS,
HOSIERY, CUTLERY,

HATS, CAPS, TRUNKS, &c.,

NO. 13 MARKET STREET,

WILMINGTON, N. C.

C. M. VANORSDELL'S
EXTENSIVE
STOCK DEPOT,
AND
PHOTOGRAPHIC ROOMS,
No. 40½ Market Street,
WILMINGTON, N. C.

Where ARTISTS' MATERIALS of every description are sold. FRAMES, oval and square, gilt and plain, oak and walnut, of all sizes and styles, at wholesale and retail. PHOTOGRAPHIC PORTRAITURE, of every known style.— Photographs enlarged from small pictures to any desired size, and beautifully colored in oil, pastel, water and India ink.

FIRE INSURANCE,
IN THE
PHŒNIX COMPANY,
OF HARTFORD, CONN.;
CITY FIRE COMPANY,
OF HARTFORD, CONN.;
HOME INSURANCE CO.,
OF NEW HAVEN, CONN.
ALL GOOD COMPANIES.
WM. L. SMITH, Agent,
OFFICE AT BANK OF WILMINGTON.

WILMINGTON DIRECTORY.

ABBREVIATIONS:

In the following pages *r* stands for residence; *bds* for boards; *bt* for between; *cor* for corner; *off* for office; *opp* for opposite; *e* for east; *w* for west; *n* for north; *s* for south; *al* for alley; *l* for lane; *nr* for near. The word *street* is implied. Numbered streets implied by the figures only; *r r* for Rail Road.

A.

Aaron, David, dry goods, 25 Market, r 3d bt Mulberry and Walnut.
Adams Express Company, off 3 Granite Row, Front street, James Macomber, Agent.
Adams, M L, engineer W & W R R, bds City Hotel.
Adkins, Mrs E, r 4th bt Ann and Nun.
Adkins, Samuel N, machinist, bds Mrs S E Adkins.
Adrian & Vollers, groceries and liquors, cor Front and Dock.
Adrian, Alex, of A & Vollers, r Dock. bt Front and Second.
Agostini, F M, confectionery, 16 Market, r cor 6th and Dock.
Ahrens, N, clk L Vollers, bds same.
Alderman, Geo F, salesman Oldham's Mill, bds n w cor 4th and Mulberry.
Alderman, Alfred, inspector naval stores, r cor 4th and Mulberry.
Alderman, I T, freight agent W, C & R R R, bds Edwin T Love.
Alderman, Archibald, inspector naval stores. r 5th st n of r r.
Alderman, James, of Bowden & A. r Red Cross, bt 3d and 4th.
Allen, J B, store cor 6th and Castle, r same.
Allen, J H, watchmaker, Brown & Anderson.
Allen, G E, printer, Herald Office, bds J F Legwin.
Allen, Wm H, treasurer and master transportation W, C & R R R, r ———.

BAILEY'S
STAR HOTEL,
FRONT STREET, WILMINGTON, N. C.

House open for the reception of guests at all hours of the day and night.

No pains will be spared to make the guests of the house comfortable in every respect.

THE TABLE

Is supplied with every luxury the market affords. A first class

RESTAURANT

Is attached to the house, where the public will be furnished with

ICE CREAM OR OYSTERS,

In their seasons; WINES, CHOICE LIQUORS, etc.

WM. H. LIPPITT,
DRUGGIST & CHEMIST,
WHOLESALE AND RETAIL.

Always on hand, a full and select supply of pure MEDICINES, CHEMICALS, DYE STUFFS, PERFUMERY, SOAPS, BRUSHES, FANCY ARTICLES, &c. &c. &c.

PRESCRIPTIONS accurately and neatly compounded.

No. 55, Market Street,
WILMINGTON, N. C.

P. S. Store open from 6 o'clock A. M., to 9 P M. Persons wishing prescriptions compounded at night, will please call at my residence on Second street, between Dock and Orange.

Aldrich, Wm, mechanic Clarendon Iron Works, r 5th bt Dock and Orange.
Alts, Fred, clk Railroad Hotel, bds same.
Altaffer, Geo M, pattern maker Hart & Bailey, r Cottage Lane, bt 3d and 4th.
Andrews, W S G, of Andrews & Bardin, r Front, bt Chesnut and Mulberry.
Andrews & Bardin, com merchants, 5 So Water, (up stairs.)
Anderson, Wm S, of Brown & Anderson, r cor Market and 5th.
Anderson, Jas & Co, commission merchants, 9 So Water.
Anderson, Jas, of Jas Anderson & Co, r Orange, bt Front and 2d.
Anderson, Alex, clk Jas Anderson & Co, bds Jas Anderson.
Anderson, E A, physician, Market, bt 2d and 3d, r cor Front and Orange.
Anderson, T W, city clerk, bds W S Anderson.
Andell, C J, salesman Geo Z French & Co.
Anke, Ernest, machinist, Hart & Bailey's, r cor 5th and Nun.
Arey, Chas R, salesman Jno Dawson, bds Jno C Bowden.
Arrington, Dr B F, dentist.
Armstrong, W T, printer, Herald Office, bds cor 7th and Mulberry.
Ashley, S S, ass't sup't Negro schools, r cor Front and Nun.
Atkinson, Roger P, sup't W, C & R R R.
Atkinson, Bishop Thomas, r Orange, bt 5th and 6th.
Atkins, Geo, clerk A E Hall, bds same.
Atkinson, Mrs Sarah, r Chesnut, bt 5th and 6th.
Atkinson & Shepperson, com merchants and insurance agents, Princess, near Water.
Atkinson, J W, of Atkinson & Shepperson, bds Orange bt 5th and 6th

B.

Baptist Church, cor Orange and 6th, Rev ———, pastor.
Baptist Church, (Front st,) Rev Mr Young, pastor.
Baptist Church, (now building,) cor Market and 5th.
Bates, E A, book-keeper M McInnis, bds R W Blancy.
Bates, Capt B G, W & M R R, r cor 4th and Walnut.
Baker, John A, lawyer.
Bailey, James H, proprietor Star Hotel, r same.
Bailey's Star Hotel, Front bt Market and Princess.
Bailey, J A, restaurant at Bailey's Hotel, r same.
Bailey, A M, clk J H Bailey, bds same.

MICHAEL CRONLY,   WILKES MORRIS.

CRONLY & MORRIS,
AUCTIONEERS & GENERAL AGENTS,

NO. 6, SOUTH WATER STREET, UP STAIRS,

WILMINGTON, N. C.

STOCKS, REAL ESTATE, and all descriptions of merchandise bought and sold on commission.

Our personal attention given to any business intrusted to our charge.

From our long experience in the business, we feel warranted in referring to the public generally.

ALEX. OLDHAM,

PROPRIETOR OF THE

Cape Fear Corn & Flour Mills,

Corner North Water and Walnut Streets.

DEALER IN GRAIN,

AND

COMMISSION MERCHANT,

No. 6, South Water Street,

WILMINGTON, N. C.

Bailey, George A, clk J A Bailey, bds same.
Bailey, John C, of Hart & Bailey, r cor 3d and Ann.
Bailey, Burt, baggage master W & W R R.
Barlow, Jos L, r Market bt 7th and 8th.
Barlow, Lewis N, agent D McEowen & Co.
Bappler, Geo P, of Hussell & Bappler, r 4th bt Chesnut and Mulberry.
Bate & Wescott, grocers, 32 Market.
Bate, R, of Bate & Wescott, r 5th, bt Walnut and Red Cross.
Barnett, S, printer Herald office, bds Market, bt 3d and 4th.
Barry, Horace M, commission merchant and wholesale grocer, and agent steamships, n Water.
Barry & Bernard, Editors and Proprietors Wilmington Dispatch, 42 Market, up stairs.
Barry, John D, of Barry & Bernard, bds cor 4th and Chesnut.
Barry, M, store Front, bt Red Cross and Campbell, r same.
Bagg, H A, bds John J Conoley.
Bank of Wilmington, Front, bt Market and Princess.
Bank of Cape Fear, Front, bt Market and Princess.
Bauman & Tienken, dealers in groceries and liquors, 22 and 24 s Front.
Bauman, John G, of Bauman & Tienken, r cor 5th and Dock.
Bauman, John C, clk H M Barry, bds Jno G Bauman.
Bauman, John, shoemaker, M Keeler, r 2d, bt Mulberry & Walnut.
Baldwin, O S, of Baldwin, Munson & Co, r 38 Market.
Baldwin, Munson & Co, clothing and gent's furnishing goods, 33 Market.
Bachman, A C, baker.
Baker, Miss Jane F, music teacher, r 2d, bt Mulberry and Walnut.
Baker, Geo, machinist, bds R H Warton.
Banks, Mrs John S, r 4th, bt Walnut and Red Cross.
Banks, Chas, clk, bds Mrs Jno S Banks.
Banks, Robert, clk Internal Rev Dept, bds Mrs Jno S Banks.
Banks, John, clk, bds Mrs Jno S Banks.
Banks, Jno S, commercial reporter Herald, bds 36 Market.
Banks, David, baggage master W & W R R.
Barnhill, Mrs A, r 3d, bt Orange and Ann.
Barclift, Mrs A H, boarding house, cor 2d and Ann.
Bauer, F L, dry goods, 23 Market.
Bell, C F, Northrop's mill, r cor 2d and Church.
Bell, Ivey P, ship carpenter, r Church, bt 2d and 3d.
Bellamy, Dr J D, r cor 5th and Market.

GEORGE HARRISS,   W. W. HARRISS,   A. J. HOWELL.

HARRISS & HOWELL,

COMMISSION MERCHANTS,

WILMINGTON, N. C.,

 AGENTS for A. C. Steamship  Line for New York; and New York, Boston, and Philadelphia Packets.

O. G. PARSLEY & CO.,

IMPORTERS

AND

COMMISSION MERCHANTS,

No. 6, North Water Street,

Wilmington, N. C.

O. G. PARSLEY, Sr.,   JOHN JUDGE,

O. G. PARSLEY, Jr.,   HENRY SAVAGE.

Bellamy, W N, bds Dr J D Bellamy.
Bettencourt, Wm H, r cor 2d and Chesnut.
Beasley, W W, printer Dispatch Office, bds 5th, bt Princess and Chesnut.
Bectol, R, machinist, W & W R R.
Bell, Wm, machinist, W & W R R.
Beach, A, blacksmith, S Burtt, r Chesnut, bt 6th and 7th.
Beckerdite, A F, watchmaker, 10 n Front.
Bernard, Wm H, of Barry & Bernard, bds City Hotel.
Bernard, P T, sup't Dispatch Office, bds City Hotel.
Beck, Thos, W & M R R, r cor 6th and Red Cross.
Berry, Wm A, physician, Front, bt Market and Princess, r 5th bt Market and Dock.
Bear, Sol & Bro, dry goods and clothing, 18 Market.
Bear, Sol, of S B & Bro. r Front, bt Mulberry and Walnut.
Bear, Sam'l, of S Bear & Bro, r Sol Bear.
Bear, Henry, clk S Bear & Bro, bds Sol Bear.
Bear, Marcus, clk S Bear & Bro, bds Sol Bear.
Bear, S & Co, dry goods and clothing, 41 and 42 n Water.
Bear, Simon, of S B & Co, r Front, bt Walnut and Mulberry.
Bear, M, agent P Newman, r 4th, bt Orange and Ann.
Beery, B W & W L, ship builders.
Beery, B W, of B W & W L B, r cor 2d and Nun.
Beery, W L, of B W & W L B, r Front, bt Ann and Nun.
Beery, Stephen W, clk W & W R R, r Red Cross, bt 2d and 3d.
Bender, D S, r Castle, bt 6th and 7th.
Bicaise, F, pressman Herald office, bds 8, bt Chesnut & Mulberry.
Biddle, Wm H, deputy sheriff and jailor, r county jail.
Bivens, W J & Co, proprietors Rock Spring Saloon, 34 n Water.
Bivens, W J, of W J B & Co, r cor 9th and Princess.
Bishop, John, butcher, Market House, r cor 5th and Ann.
Black, A D, clk Harriss & Howell, bds Mrs C C Whitney.
Blanks, Wm B, clk Murray & Murchison, bds Mrs C K Price.
Blancy, Mrs E, school teacher, r Dock, bt 2d and 3d.
Blaney, R W B, money clerk Express Office, r cor 2d and Ann.
Bloom, Peter, of Lutzen & B, r N Water, bt Walnut and Red Cross.
Blumenthal, Mrs H, dry goods, 3 n Front, r 2d bt Ann and Nun.
Blumenthal, S & Co, dry goods, &c, cor Front and Market.
Blumenthal, S, of S B & Co, r 4th, bt Chesnut and Mulberry.
Blum, Peter, shoemaker J J Gay, r 6th, bt Nun and Church.
Blackman, Capt H B, U S A Q M, cor Princess and Water, r cor 3d and Nun.

HOUSE, SIGN,
ORNAMENTAL,
AND
FRESCO PAINTING
DONE IN THE MOST APPROVED STYLE,
AND AT THE LOWEST RATES,
BY
MADISON & THOMSON,
Princess Street, between Front and Water,
WILMINGTON, N. C.

JACOB LYON,
Nos. 1 and 2, Corner of Market and Water Streets,
WILMINGTON, N. C.
STAPLE AND FANCY DRY GOODS,
AND
MANUFACTURER OF CLOTHING.

A LARGE STOCK OF
BOOTS, SHOES, HATS, CAPS, AND GENT'S FURNISHING
GOODS; ALSO, CUTLERY.

Blossom, Jos R & Co, com merchants, Dock, bt Front and Water.
Blossom, Sam'l, store, cor 5th and Church, r cor 6th and Castle.
Bloom, II H, store cor 5th and Chesnut, r same.
Bond, Henry, clk Henry McLin, bds same.
Bowden, Wm N. r cor 3d and Chesnut.
Bowden, Jno C, inspector naval stores, r cor 2d and Chesnut.
Bowden, W B, bds Jno C Bowden.
Bowden & Alderman, inspectors timber and lumber, 34 N Water, up stairs.
Bowden, Jas O, inspector naval stores, r Red Cross, bt 3d and 4th.
Bowden, L H, of B & Alderman, r Princess, bt 4th and 5th.
Bowden, Jos N, baggage master W & M R R, r cor Princess and 4th.
Bohling, Martin, clerk H M Bremer, bds same.
Borden, J C, conductor W & W R R, bds R R Hotel.
Borden, Wm H, clk A Davids & Co, bds W B Edmondson.
Boney, C, machinist W & W R R, bds P Dahmer.
Bradley & Woehler, commission merchants and agents commercial line steamships, North Water.
Bradley, David C, of B & Woehler.
Bradley, Dr A O, physician, Front, bt Dock and Orange, r same.
Bradley, James A. r cor 7th and Chesnut.
Braddy, Wm, bds Mrs A Barnhill.
Bryan, Henry, engineer W & M R R, bds R R Hotel.
Brown & Anderson, watches and jewelry, 37 Market.
Brown, T W, of B & Anderson, r Orange, bt Front and 2d.
Brown, Jno B, salesman S M Simpson, bds Miles Costin.
Brown. E A, express messenger, bds ———
Brown, Asa, express messenger, bds ———
Brown, R W, printer Dispatch office, bds Market, bt 7th and 8th.
Brown, Jno Kent, of James & B, r ———
Brown, A D, salesman Kahnweiler & Bro, bds Ann, bt 2d and 3d.
Browning, E D, conductor W & W R R, bds Jas Lumsden.
Brown, K, cooper, r Market, bt 7th and 8th.
Brickhouse, N E, r cor Front and Church
Bremer, J, grocer, 50 and 52 Market, r same.
Bremer, H, clerk J Bremer, bds same.
Bremer, J M, of Stolter & Bremer, r N E cor Market and 2d.
Bremer, N, grocer, cor Front and Church, r same.
Bremer, II M, groceries and liquors, cor Front and Dock, r same.
Bryant, J, mechanic Hart & Bailey's, bds Chesnut, bt Front and 2d.
Buie, James E, r Nun, bt 2d and 3d.
Buie, D A, physician, r 2d, bt Ann and Nun.

D. A. SMITH,

WHOLESALE AND RETAIL GROCER,

AND DEALER IN

Furniture, Looking-Glasses,

CHINA, GLASS AND EARTHEN WARE,

WOOD AND WILLOW WARE,

&c., &c., &c.,

Nos. 26 and 28 South Front St.,

WILMINGTON, N. C.

Buie, Miss Mary Ann, soldiers' friend, r ——.
Burr, Jas G, cashier Bank Cape Fear, r Bank building.
Burr, C E & Co, ornamental and sign painters, Front, bt Dock and Orange.
Burr, C E, of C E B & Co, r cor 8th and Market.
Burr, A B, of C E Burr & Co, r 5th, bt Market and Princess.
Burr, H, salesman S M Simpson, r Dock, bt Front and 2d.
Burr, H C, salesman, S M Simpson, bds H Burr.
Burtt, S, blacksmith, Mulberry, bt Front and Water. r 4th, bt Market and Dock.
Burtt, S, Jr, clk M M Katz, bds S Burtt.
Burriss, Thos E, pilot, r Church, bt 4th and 5th.
Burkhimer, Henry, tobacco, cigars, &c, 6th Market, r S E cor 4th and Ann.
Burkhimer, W, r Cottage Lane, bt 3d and 4th.
Burkhead, Rev L S, pastor Front st M E Church, r cor 2d and Walnut
Burnet, Thos B, hunter, r cor 5th and Queen.
Bunting, S R, r 5th, bt Market and Dock.
Bunting & Yopp, provision inspectors, 24 North Water, (up stairs.)
Bunting, D E, of B & Yopp, r 3d, bt Red Cross and Campbell.
Bulcken, J G, clerk Adrian & Vollers, r Orange, bt 4th and 5th.
Burch, W F. r —— al, bt 2d and 3d.
Byrd, Martha, r —— al, bt 8th and 9th.

C.

Calder, R E, book-keeper Shackelford, Haas & Co, r cor Market and 6th.
Calder, W, clk W & M R R, r cor Market and 6th.
Caldwell, W J, printer Herald off, bds Market, bt 3d and 4th.
Cantwell, Jno L, freight agent W & M R R, bds Mrs C K Price.
Capps, A, mechanic, Hart & Bailey's, r cor 6th and Castle.
Carpenter, A, salesman, J S Topham & Co, bds 5th, bt Dock and Orange.
Carr, N, clk R F Eyden, r 5th, bt Hanover and Brunswick.
Carr, Thos B, dentist, 45½ Market, r same.
Casey, J N, carpenter, r Walnut, bt 3d and 4th.
Cassidey, J, ship-builder, S Water, r Church, bt Front and Water.
Cazaux, A D, commercial reporter Dispatch office, bds City Hotel.
Chadbourn, Jas H & Co, commission merchants and steam saw mill, off Dock, bt Front and Water.

M. COHN.   J. D. RYTTENBERG.

COHN & RYTTENBERG,

WHOLESALE AND RETAIL DEALERS IN

 STAPLE AND FANCY DRY GOODS,

OF ALL KINDS,

MILLINERY, CLOTHS, CASSIMERES,

SATINETS, CLOTHING, HATS, CAPS,

 Boots, Shoes,

AND

Gentlemen's Furnishing Goods,

33 Market Street,

WILMINGTON, N. C.,

AND

Smith's Corner, Fayetteville St.,

RALEIGH, N. C.

Dealers will find it the cheapest and best assorted and selected stock in the market.

FRESH GOODS received by every steamer.

Chadbourn, Jas H, of J H C & Co, r Orange, bt 3d and 4th.
Chadbourn, Geo, of J H C & Co, r Orange, bt 3d and 4th.
Charles, J G, printer Journal off, bds J F Legwin.
Chesnut, C L, book-keeper, Cox, Kendall & Co.
Cherry, F, tailor.
City Hall, cor Princess and 3d.
City Hotel, Frederick & Shemwell, proprietors, cor 2d and Market.
Clark, J M, clerk Worth & Daniel, bds cor Front and Dock.
Clark, Wm M, carpenter, r Chesnut, bt 4th and 5th.
Cohn & Ryttenberg, dry goods and clothing, 43 Market.
Corbin, L, dentist, Front, bt Market and Dock, r R Morris.
Corbet, W J, clerk A R Storer, r Hanover, bt 2d and 3d.
Corbett, Jas T, clk Herald office, bds 3d, bt Walnut and Red Cross.
Cornehlsen, J H N, bds Jas Lumsden.
Collins, James W, accountant A Oldham, r cor 5th and Orange.
Collison, W C, bds cor 3d and Red Cross.
Colville, T L, foreman Hart & Bailey's, bds Mrs W G Milligan.
Coney, John R, r 3d, bt Orange and Ann.
Conner, David, carpenter, W & W R R, bds S G Northrop.
Conoley, John J, special magistrate, r Market, bt 4th and 5th.
Cook, Thos M & Co, proprietors Wilmington Herald, 36 Market.
Cook, Thos M, of T M C & Co, r cor Dock and 2d.
Cook, J C, store cor 3d and Nun, r same.
Cooper, John, mechanic Hart & Bailey's, r 2d, bt Market and Dock.
Copes, Mrs B F, r cor 6th and Chesnut.
Copes, Geo S, cabinet maker, 2d bt Market and Princess, bds S W Roberts.
Copes, B F, clk James Lumsden, bds same.
Costin, A J, clk, bds Miles Costin.
Costin, Mrs John, r Dock, bt 6th and 7th.
Costin, W T, clk Wm Porter, bds Wm H Costin.
Costin, Wm H, brick mason, r cor 6th and Nun.
Costin, Miles, cor 5th and Dock.
County Jail, Princess, bt 3d and 4th.
Court House, Princess, bt 2d and 3d.
Cowan, Mrs Sarah, r cor 4th and Chesnut.
Cowan, R H, President W, C & R R R.
Cowan, Platt D, clk Dispatch Office, bds Mrs S Cowan.
Cowan, John, conductor W, C & R R R, bds Mrs S Cowan.
Cowan, Mrs John, r cor Front and Mulberry.
Cox, Kendall & Co, commission merchants and wholesale grocers, 23 N Water.

ELIJAH WILLIS,
DRUGGIST AND CHEMIST,
DEALER IN

Drugs, Select Medicines, English and German Chemicals, Fancy Articles, Perfumery, Seed, and Patent Medicines of all kinds.

IRON FRONT STORE,
Market Street, Wilmington, N. C.

N. B. PRESCRIPTIONS carefully compounded.

Persons wishing medicines at night, will call on Mr. Shaffer, one door West of the Journal office.

ALFRED MARTIN,
COMMISSION AND FORWARDING MERCHANT,
AND MANUFACTURER OF
ROSIN OIL, NAPTHA, PITCH
SPIRITS TURPENTINE AND ROSIN,
Office No. 5 South Water St.,
WILMINGTON, N. C.

S. M. WEST,
AUCTIONEER
AND
Commission Merchant,
No. 6 South Water Street,
WILMINGTON, N. C.

Cox, J J, of C, Kendall & Co, r ———.
Cox, John, printer Herald office, bds G Prigge.
Cronly & Morris, auctioneers and general agents, 6 S Water, up stairs.
Cronly, Michael, of C & Morris, bds John A Taylor.
Craig, J G, gunsmith A H Neff, r 8th, bt Mulberry and Walnut.
Craft, Mrs T C, r Princess, bt 8th and 9th.
Craft, T C, Jr, clk D A Smith, bds mrs T C Craft.
Craig, John B, tailor, r Princess, bt 4th and 5th.
Craffy, M, gardener, E Kidder, r 4th, bt Dock and Orange.
Custom House, N Water, bt Market and Princess.
Cumming, James D, book-keeper J H Chadbourn & Co, r Orange, bt 4th and 5th.
Cumming, Wm A.
Currie, S A & Co, livery stables, cor 2d and Princess.
Currie, S A, of S A C & Co, r at stables.
Currie, John K, r Market street continuation.
Cutlar, F J, physician, off over Bank of Wilmington, r cor 2d and Walnut.
Cutlar, DuBrutz, attorney at law, r 2d, bt Walnut and Red Cross.
Cutts, A H, conductor W & W R R, bds City Hotel.

D.

Daggett, W T, salesman H C Elliott.
Dahmer, J, store cor Water and Red Cross, r same.
Dahmer, P, store Water, bt Red Cross and Walnut, r same.
Daniel, N G, of Worth & D, r cor 2d and Ann.
Daniels, Thos, proprietor Mechanic's Hotel, r same.
Darby, James, sup't Gas Light Co, r cor Church and Surry.
David, Aaron & Co, clothing, 53 Market.
Davis, J T, clerk Cohn & Ryttenberg, bds Mrs C C Whitney.
Davis, James, clerk Harriss & Howell, bds Mrs C C Whitney.
Davis, John, tragedian and leading man Wilmington Theatre, bds City Hotel.
Dawson, John, dry goods and hardware, 19 and 21 Market.
Dawson, John, mayor of city, r 2d, bt Market and Dock.
Dawson, James, broker, 28 Market, r cor Front and Chesnut.
Dawson, Geo, machinist W & W R R, bds ———.
Daymon & Johnson, cabinet makers and undertakers, cor 2d and Market, up stairs.
Daymon, Jno C, of D & Johnson, r Castle, bt 5th and 6th.

D. G. WORTH. N. G. DANIEL.

WORTH & DANIEL,
COMMISSION and FORWARDING MERCHANTS,
BROWN'S WHARVES,
South Water Street, Wilmington, N. C.

Will give strict personal attention to sale or shipment of
Cotton, Naval Stores and General Produce,
Also, to receiving and forwarding Goods: Agents for Cape Fear Line of River Steamers to Fayetteville, and Sail Lines to New York and Philadelphia.

Dealers in Cotton, Bagging, Rope, Lime, Plaster, Guano, Ford's Fertilizer, Salt, Coal, &c.

ISHAM PETERSON,
WITH
C. M. HALL,
Wholesale and Retail Dealer in

DRY GOODS, BOOTS, SHOES, FUR, WOOL AND
FELT HATS,
No. 29 MARKET STREET,
(HEDRICK & RYAN'S OLD STAND,)
WILMINGTON, N. C.

Country Merchants would do well to examine our stock before purchasing elsewhere.

Orders promptly attended to.

Davis, Wm E, r Chesnut, bt 8th and 9th.
Day & Wright, drug store, 71 Market.
Day, W E, of D & Wright, r Market bt 2d and 3d.
Dean, Jas, book-keeper Kidder & Martin, r Ann, bt 2d and 3d.
Delaney, D, tailor, r Market, bt 8th and 9th.
DeBebian, Mrs —, boarding house, r 2d, bt Princess and Chesnut.
DeRosset, A J, commission merchant, r cor 2d and Dock.
DeRosset, A L. clerk internal revenue dep't, bds A J DeRosset.
DeNeale, Mrs W H, r 47 Market, up stairs.
DeNeale, Wm H, Jr, bds Mrs DeNeale.
Deumeland, A, grocer, cor Dock and Water, r same.
Dickinson, P K, r cor Front and Chesnut.
Dicksey, J W, clerk W N Peden, bds N E Brickhouse.
Dicksey, J J, r 4th, bt Nun and Church.
Dienstbach, W, r Front, bt Market and Dock.
Divine, John F, master machinist W & W R R, r 4th, n of R R.
Donally, T, sup't Oakdale Cemetery, r cor Princess and 9th.
Dodd, Wm, clerk S VanAmringe, bds 2d, bt Ann and Nun.
Doughtery, P, clerk James McCormick, bds same.
Drane, Henry M, sup't W & M R R, r cor 5th and Chesnut.
Driscoll and Kerrigan, proprietors Wilmington House, Toomer's al, bt Front and 2d.
Driscoll, D, of D & Kerrigan, r Wilmington House.
Dudley & Bro, general insurance agents, 5 s Water, up stairs.
Dudley, Edward B, of D & Bro, r Market, bt 7th and 8th.
Dudley, Robert C, of D & Bro, r Market, bt 7th and 8th.
Dudley, Guilford L, freight agent W & W R R, bds A Martin.
Dunlap, W, works M Barry, bds same.
Duse, Chas, store cor Water and Red Cross, r same.
Dunden, Thos, clerk Geo Z French & Co.
Dugid, W H, carpenter W & W R R, r 8th, bt Mulberry & Walnut.
Dyer, Jno, cutter Baldwin, Munson & Co, r cor Market and 10th.
Dymott, R E, gas fitter Hart & Bailey's, bds Jas H Mitchell.
Dyer, S, clk G W Williams, bds same.

E.

Earpe, C, r Chesnut, bt 4th and 5th.
Eckel, H, grocer, cor Front and Dock, r same.
Edmondson, W B, com merch, cor Front and Red Cross, r same.
Egan, P & Co, groceries and liquors, 46 N Water.
Egan, P, of P Egan & Co, bds Princess, bt Front and Water.

L. FLANAGAN,
FANCY AND VARIETY STORE,
No. 23 So. FRONT STREET.

(MRS. BOYD'S OLD STAND,)

DEALER IN

MILLINERY, TOYS, FRUITS, CONFECTIONERIES
AND FANCY GOODS
OF ALL KINDS.

Keeps constantly on hand a handsome and well assorted stock of everything usually found in a fancy store. The lady so well known to the public as Mrs. BOYD, is in charge of the Millinery department, where she will be pleased to attend to the wants of all her old friends and customers.

HORACE M. BARRY,
NORTH WATER STREET,
WILMINGTON, N. C.,

COMMISSION MERCHANT

AND WHOLESALE DEALER IN

Groceries, Provisions
AND

GENERAL PRODUCE.

CASH advances made on consignments to ARTHUR LEARY, N. Y.

Agent for Steamships

STARLIGHT and COMMANDER.

Egan, E J, of P E & Co, bds cor 5th and Princess.
Eilers, H B, commission merchant and grocer, cor Market and S Water. r cor 5th and Orange.
Eilers, W T, clk Hart & Bailey, bds H B Eilers.
Eilers, E H, clk Worth & Daniel, bds H B Eilers.
Ellis & Mitchell, grain dealers, 9 N Water.
Ellis, C D, of E & Mitchell, bds Mrs Henry P Russell.
Ellis, C S, of Russell & E, bds Mrs Henry P Russell.
Ellis, A, r 2d, bt Orange and Ann.
Ellis, James H, carpenter W & W R R, r cor 3d and Walnut.
Elliot, H C, hardware and general merckandize, 7 Market.
Elwell, Mrs Wm, r cor 3d and Walnut.
Elwell, Eli, book-binder P Heinsberger, bds Mrs Wm Elwell.
Empie, Adam, attorney at law, off Journal buildings, r Front, bt Ann and Nun.
Episcopal Church, St. James', cor Market and 3d, Rev A A Watson, pastor.
Episcopal Church, St. John's, cor 3d and Red Cross, Rev R H Terry, pastor.
Episcopal Church, St. Paul's, cor 4th and Orange, Rev Geo Patterson, officiating.
Ertkenker, I F, physician, cor Market and 2d, r 4th, bt Ann & Nun.
Evans, J J, conductor W & M R R, r ——.
Evans, Thos, book-keeper J R Blossom & Co.
Evans, Henry C, clk G R French & Son, bds G R French.
Everett, Mrs A M, r 7th, bt Chesnut and Mulberry.
Everett, Jno A, clk Smith & Strauss, bds Mrs A M Everett.
Eyden, F, store cor 5th and Walnut, r same.

F.

Fanning, P W, sign painter, Front, bt Orange and Ann, r same.
Faulkner, J R & Co, proprietors Railroad Hotel, cor Front and Red Cross.
Faulkner, J R, of J R F & Co, r Railroad Hotel.
Farmers' House, Water, bt Mulberry and Walnut.
Fees, George G, watchmaker F W Knohl, bds same.
Fergus, Daniel, r 2d, bt Ann and Nun.
Ferrand, Miss Sallie, transient boarding house, r 3d, bt Ann & Nun.
Fitzgerald, John, butcher, r Princess, bt Water and Front.
Fitzgerald M, clerk, Red Cross, bt Front and 2d.

S. M. SIMPSON,

WHOLESALE DEALER AND JOBBER IN

DRY GOODS,

READY-MADE CLOTHING,

FELT AND WOOL HATS,

Boots and Shoes, Notions, &c.,

33 and 35 Market Street,

—AND—

2 and 4 Front Street, N. E. Corner.

CONFINING OURSELVES STRICTLY TO THE

JOBBING TRADE.

And having the various departments well stocked, Merchants will find it to their interest to call.

GOODS sold at New York market rates, with expenses added.

Finger, John F, clerk Kidder & Martin's mill, r same.
Fillyaw, Mrs O L, r 4th, bt Harnet and Bladen.
Flanner, Wm B, commission and forwarding merchant, and agent Murray's line sailing packets, r Front, bt Walnut and Red Cross
Flanner, Henry G, clerk W B Flanner, bds same.
Flanner, C, local reporter for Journal office, bds W B Flanner.
Flanner, B, clerk Murray & Murchison, bds W B Flanner.
Flanagan, L, variety store, 21 and 23 S Front, r same.
Flanagan, Dennis, r Princess, bt Water and Front.
Fleet, James, r cor 5th and Nun.
Flowers, John, r Walnut, bt 7th and 8th.
Foley, Terrence V, of T M Cook & Co, r 36 Market.
Fox, Geo A, enginneer, r 6th, bt Chesnut and Mulberry.
Forrest, John J, seaman, r cor 4th and Church.
Fowler, W G, r cor Front and Ann.
Fowler, N R, r Front, bt Church and Nun.
Fowler, W G Jr, bds N R Fowler.
Fowler, N R, Jr, machinist, bds N R Fowler.
Foyles, Mrs D M, r cor 7th and Dock.
Freeman, William E, physician, Front, bt Chesnut and Mulberry, r same.
Fremont, Col S L, sup't W & W R R, r cor Front and Walnut.
French, Geo Z & Co, groceries and liquors, 10 S Front.
French, Geo Z, of G Z F & Co, bds ——
French, C H, salesman Geo Z French & Co.
French, Wm R, clerk W, C & R R R, bds C E Burr.
French, R S, of Person & French.
French, Geo R & Son, boots and shoes, 11 Market.
French, Geo R, of Geo R French & Son, r cor 4th and Dock.
French, Wm A, of G R French & Son, r 4th, bt Dock & Orange.
French, Geo R, Jr, clerk G R French & Son, bds G R French.
French, J McD, clerk G R French & Son, bds G R French.
French, Chas B, bds G R French.
Frederick & Shemwell, proprietors City Hotel.
Fulton & Price, proprietors Wilmington Journal, Journal Buildings, Princess, bt Front and 2d.
Fulton, Jas, of Fulton & Price, Editor Journal, r 4th, bt Princess and Chesnut.
Fulton, Mrs C A, r 4th, bt Princess and Chesnut.
Furlong, Walter, proprietor Wilmington ice house, Dock, bt Front and Water, r 2d, bt Market and Princess.

HUSSELL & BAPPLER,

Wholesale and Retail Dealers in

ALES, WINES, LIQUORS,

Cigars and Tobacco,

GROCERIES,

DRY GOODS AND FANCY GOODS,

Buyers of Produce generally.

CORNER OF WATER AND MULBERRY STS.,

WILMINGTON, N. C.

C. HUSSELL,   G. P. BAPPLER

G.

Gadsby, James H, clk S Kelley, bds J Meier.
Gadsby, J E, city baggage express.
Ganzer, C H, clerk H M Barry.
Gardner, Junius D, Sr,. r Mulberry bt 4th and 5th.
Gardner, T M, Custom House, r Market bt 6th and 7th.
Gardner, J D, Jr, clk M McInnis, bds J W Collins.
Gardner, Geo G, engineer W, C & R R R.
Garrity, Jas H, moulder W & W R R, r N of R R.
Gates, Geo W, machinist W & W R R.
Gay, J J, shoemaker, cor 3d and Orange, r cor 3d and Walnut.
Gerkin, H, store cor 6th and Mulberry, r same.
Gerkin, N, grocer, Princess bt Front and Water,
Gerguson, P, blacksmith Hart & Bailey, r Dock bt 7th and 8th.
Gillespie. Geo S, com merchant, S Water, bds F C Singletary.
Gilbert, Henry D, clk Custom House, r 5th bt Dock and Orange.
Gilligan, Charles, r ——— al, bt 8th and 9th.
Goteberg, N, variety store 46 Market, r cor Princess and 2d.
Gorman, J W, clk H Webb, bds same.
Goodman, S, clk S Bear & Bro.
Grady, B F, exchange broker, cor Water and Princess, bds City Hotel.
Grant, F, clk City Hotel, bds same.
Grant, Rev Reuben, r 5th bt Ann and Nun.
Grant, James, r cor Market and 7th.
Grainger, I B, book-keeper James Dawson, bds same.
Greene, Z H, commission merchant and grocer, 4 N Water.
Green, James G, W & M R R, r cor Nun and 2d.
Green, Samuel, bds Mrs J J Lippitt.
Greenburg, R, salesman J Newman, bds same.
Greer, David J, r 2d bt Orange and Ann.
Greer, John, bds D J Greer.
Greer, T C, telegraph operator, bds D J Greer.
Griffith, John, assistant chief police, r cor 6th and Castle.
Groetjen, Wm, grocer, cor Front and Church, r same.
Groves, Mrs S A, r cor 7th and Mulberry.

H.

Haas, Sol, of Shackelford, Haas & Co, r ———.
Hall, E D, r Front bt Market and Princess.
Hall, Dr Wm H, r cor Market and 3d.

S. D. WALLACE,   J. B. SOUTHERLAND.

Wallace & Southerland,

GENERAL
COMMISSION MERCHANTS,

OFFICE NO. 24, NORTH WATER STREET,

WHARVES AND WAREHOUSES FOOT OF WALNUT STREET,

WILMINGTON, N. C.,

Will give prompt personal attention to all consignments of

Naval Stores, Cotton,

SPIRITS TURPENTINE, ROSIN,

TAR, PROVISIONS, &c. &c.,

either for sale or shipment. Also, to forwarding merchandize, &c.

Agents Greensboro' Mutual Insurance Company.

Hall, A E, com mer, 22 N Water, r 5th bt Dock and Orange.
Hall, C M, dry goods, 29 Market, bds I Peterson.
Hall, Watson, r Church bt Front and 2d.
Hallett, B A, distillery opposite city, bds City Hotel.
Hanchey, O R, store cor Market and 7th.
Hanchey, Henry, tailor Baldwin, Munson & Co, r Front bt Chesnut and Mulberry.
Hancock, E T, salesman N Jacobi & Co, bds City Hotel.
Hannon, —, policeman, r Chesnut bt 5th and 6th.
Hansley, E, r cor 7th and Walnut.
Hartz, H, dry goods and clothing, 17 Market, r same.
Harrison, B P, clk Baldwin, Munson & Co, bds H H Munson.
Harriss & Howell, com and forwarding merchants, N Water.
Harriss, George, of H & Howell, r 2d bt Dock and Orange.
Harriss, W W, of H & Howell, r 2d bt Princess and Chesnutt.
Harriss, W M, clk Worth & Daniel, r Market bt 9th and 10th.
Harris, R L, mechanic Hart & Bailey's, bds G M Altaffer.
Hardwick, J M, of Larkins & H, r Princess bt 8th and 9th.
Hartsfield, A A, r cor 7th and Market.
Hartsfield, W B, coppersmith W & W R R, r cor 3d & Campbell.
Hart, L A, of H & Bailey, r 3d bt Dock and Orange.
Harrell, W H, clk F M Agostini, bds same.
Harrell, E J, of King & H, r Mulberry bt 8th and 9th.
Hardy, Wm H, clk D A Smith, r cor 3d and Craig's al.
Hashagen, H, store cor 4th and Walnut, r same.
Hauft, C, shoemaker.
Hawkins, John, carpenter Daymon & Johnson, r 5th bt Castle and Queen.
Hawkins, J J, boot and shoemaker, r 5th bt Dock and Orange.
Hawes, C W, bds cor 4th and Princess.
Hays, Wm M, printer Journal office, r Walnut bt 2d and 3d.
Haynie, Wm, conductor W & M R R, bds City Hotel.
Hebert, V A, book keeper Cohn & Rytenberg.
Hedrick & Ryan, wholesale and retail dry goods, 5 and 7 N Front, next door South of Cape Fear Bank.
Hedrick, John J, of H & Ryan, r Princess, bt Front and 2d.
Heins, J F, groceries and liquors, 44 N Water, r same.
Heinsberger, P, bookbinder and blank book manufacturer, Journal buildings, r F W Knohl.
Heinsberger, Edward, clk J Newman, bds same.
Henman, B P, clk Hopkins & Johnstone, bds Mrs Lewis.
Henning, Robt, wood yard, Cassidey's wharf, bds Jas Cassidey.

WILLIAM PATTEN,
BAKERY,

44 Market Street,
Wilmington, N. C.

Keeps constantly on hand a large supply of the best
Fresh Breakfast Rolls, Tea Rolls, Bread, Cakes, Pies,
FRESH SODA, BUTTER AND ARROW ROOT CRACKERS,
PILOT BREAD, &c. &c.
All orders for CAKES. &c., for weddings and parties, will be executed in the most approved manner and at the shortest notice.

CITY HOTEL,

N. W. CORNER MARKET AND SECOND STREETS,

WILMINGTON, N. C.

FREDERICK & SHEMWELL,

PROPRIETORS.

N. FREDERICK,   P. SHEMWELL.

Herring, J C, clk Hopkins & Johnstone, bds Mrs Lewis.
Herring, M, works Globe Saloon, bds same.
Hewlet, John H, machinist, bds Mrs Lewis.
Hewlet & Kennedy, grocers, cor Front and Castle.
Hewlet, E D, of H & Kennedy, r Castle bt 6th and 7th.
Hewett, John H, boot and shoemaker, cor Market and 2d, up stairs, r cor 5th and Church.
Heyer & Ulrich, grocers, N Water.
Heyer, F W, of H & Ulrich.
Highsmith, Wm, blacksmith, 10th bt Princess and Market, r cor Princess and 12th.
Hill, James H, book-keeper Shackelford, Haas & Co, r Front bt Market and Princess.
Hill, Gaston, clk P Newman, r cor Church and 7th.
Hines, John, policeman, r cor Market and 7th.
Hines, John, grocer, cor 8th and Walnut.
Hodges, John A, printer Herald office, bds cor 9th and Princess.
Holden, S W, clk James Wilson, r Princess bt 8th and 9th.
Holmes, John L, attorney at law, office at Court House, r cor 4th and Chesnut.
Hopkins & Johnstone, groceries and crockery, 2 Granite Row, Front bt Market and Dock.
Hopkins, J M, of H & Johnstone, bds Princess bt Front and 2d.
Horen, M, grocer, 47 N Water, r same.
Horning, Geo T, engineer steamer Gen'l Howard, bds W Aldrich.
Hoskins, Mrs M, r Orange bt 2d and 3d.
Howell, A J, of Harris & H, r cor 2d and Dock.
Howey, T H, city tax collector, r cor 4th and Ann.
Howland, S, clk W T Huggins, r cor 7th and Mulberry.
Howland, J L, printer Herald office, bds Market bt 3d and 4th.
Huff & Wright, carpenters, cor Front and Ann.
Huff, J H, of H & Wright, r Ann bt Front and 2d.
Huggins, W T, groceries, &c, 54 and 56 Market, r 4th bt Dock and Orange.
Huggins, Geo W, jeweller Brown & Anderson's, bds cor 7th and Mulberry.
Hughes, J C, policeman, r Market bt 7th and 8th.
Hussell & Bappler, groceries and liquors, cor Water and Mulberry.
Hussell, C, of H & Bappler, r cor 5th and Mulberry.
Hutaf, Henry, grocer, 39 N Water, r same
Hutaf, John, clk H Hutaf, bds same.
Hyslop, J, pressman Herald office, r 3d bt Red Cross and Walnut.

J. MEIER,

DOCK STREET, BETWEEN FRONT AND WATER,

WILMINGTON, N. C.,

DEALER IN

Lager Beer, French Brandy,

OLD RYE

AND

BOURBON WHISKEY,

RUM, GIN, &c.

With the finest assortment of Wines in the market.

I.

Irvine, J W, groceries, &c, 2 N Water, r same.
Ivey, John R. conductor W & W R R, bds City Hotel.
Ivey, S P, r Market street continued.

J.

Jacobs, Wm L, harness maker, r cor 4th and Princess.
Jacobs, B J, saddlery and harness, 69 Market, r Princess, bt 4th and 5th.
Jacobi, N & Co, dry goods, 9 Market.
James & Brown, civil engineers and surveyors, next west Journal Buildings.
James, Wm H, of James & Brown.
James, John S, inspector naval stores, r 32 Market, up stairs.
James, J T, bds John S James.
James, T C, bds John S James.
James, John C, clerk Journal Office, bds John S James.
James, F M. brick mason, r cor 8th and Old Boundary.
Jenkins & Bro, cabinet makers and undertakers, Princess, bt Water and Front.
Jenkins, C H, of Jenkins & Bro, bds H M Jenkins.
Jenkins, H M, manager Theatre, r 4th, bt Princess and Chesnut.
Jewett, G W, school, cor 2d and Chesnut.
Johnston, T J, commission merchant S Water, r Market, bt 6th and 7th.
Johnson, R M, of Dayman & Johnson, bds J C Dayman.
Johnson, Thos H, butcher Market House, r cor 7th and Dock.
Johnson, A J, butcher, r 7th, bt Chesnut and Mulberry.
Johnson, policemen, bds M Barry.
Johnstone, E W, of Hopkins & Johnstone, bds Princess, bt Front and 2d.
Jones, Richard J, sheriff, r Market, bt 8th and 9th.
Jones, Miss Carrie, r 5th, bt Dock and Orange.
Jones, Willie, bds Miss Carrie Jones.
Jones, J L, printer Journal Office, bds cor 7th and Mulberry.
Judge, John, of O G Parsley & Co, r ———.

K.

Kahn, D clerk Marcus & Kehr, bds H Marcus.

WILMINGTON BAR,

A. R. STORER, Proprietor,

NO. 10, MARKET STREET,

WILMINGTON, N. C.

BEST of WINES, LIQUORS and HAVANA CIGARS.

 **NEW RIVER OYSTERS,**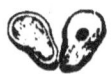

WHEN IN SEASON.

DAYMON & JOHNSON,

Corner Market and Second Streets, up stairs,

WILMINGTON, N. C.,

CABINET MAKERS

AND

Undertakers.

HOUSE, SIGN & SHIP PAINTERS,

AND

GRAINERS.

JOHN C. DAYMON, R. M. JOHNSON.

Kahnweiler & Bro, millinery, dry goods, shoes, clothing, &c, S W cor Front and Market.
Kahnweiler, Daniel, of Kahnweiler & Bro, r S W cor Front and Market.
Kahnweiler, Emanuel, clerk Kahnweiler & Bro, bds S W cor Front and Market.
Katz, M M, dry goods and clothing, 23 Market.
Keele, H, store 4th, bt Walnut and Red Cross, r same.
Keeler, M, boot and shoe maker, Princess, bt Front and Water, r same.
Keen, Jos L, brickmason, r cor 5th and Princess.
Kehr, A, of Marcus & Kehr, bds H Marcus.
Keith, E A, commission merchant, 5 S Water, r Orange, bt 3d and 4th.
Kelley, Stephen, saloon 18 N Water, r same.
Kelley, Oliver, clerk Zeno H Greene.
Kelley, Wm H, clerk Shackelford, Haas & Co, bds J Shackelford.
Kelley, J, carpenter James F Post, bds P Gergusen.
Kelley, Ann B, r —— al, bt 8th and 9th.
Kendall, Wm P, Jr, of Cox, Kendall & Co, bds Jno C Bowden.
Kendrick, James, printer Dispatch Office, bds 5th, bt Princess and Chesnut.
Kendrick, F F, book-keeper Geo Z French & Co.
Kennedy, John, mechanic Hart & Bailey, bds Queen, bt 4th and 5th.
Kennedy, R, printer Journal Office, bds C F Bell.
Kennedy, D R, of Hewlett & K, r Front, bt Church and Castle.
Kerrigan, J, of Driscoll & K, r Wilmington House.
Keyser, Jacob, bootmaker, r 9th, bt Princess and Chesnut.
Kidder & Martin, commission merchants, insurance agents, and proprietors of the Cowan steam saw and planing mills, office cor Dock and Water, (up stairs.)
Kidder, E, of Kidder & Martin, r cor 3d and Dock.
Kinder, Thos D, painter W & W R R, bds P Dalimer.
King & Harrell, grocers, 48 Market.
King, A J, of King & Harrell, r cor Princess and 9th.
King, F M, book-keeper Andrews & Bardin, bds cor 4th & Queen.
King, James, of Mallard & King, bds L H Bowden.
King, F W, clerk N Goteberg, bds A J King.
King, Jere J, butcher, r 2d, bt Nun and Church.
King, Jere, butcher, bds Jere J King.
King, John B, butcher Market House, 1 Wooster, bt 8th nd 9th.

H. M. JENKINS,   C. H. JENKINS.

JENKINS & BROTHER,

PRINCESS, BETWEEN WATER and FRONT STS.,

WILMINGTON, N. C.,

 **CABINET MAKERS**

AND

UNDERTAKERS,

Will execute all orders in the most approved style, and at the lowest rates.

P. EGAN,   E. J. EGAN.

P. EGAN & CO.,

WHOLESALE AND RETAIL DEALERS IN

GROCERIES, PROVISIONS,

WINES, LIQUORS, CIGARS, &c.

NO. 46, NORTH WATER STREET,

WILMINGTON, N. C.

COTTON AND NAVAL STORES

Bought or received on consignment.

King, J Francis, physician, 69 Market, (up stairs.)
Kirkland, John A, local reporter Wilmington Herald, bds Bailey's Hotel.
Klander, L, manufacturer ginger pop, &c, cor Front and Church, r same.
Kling, Fred, painter, bds J G Voss.
Knight, A P, policeman, r Church, bt 2d and 3d.
Knohl, F W, watchmaker and jeweller, 9 S Front, r 5th, bt Market and Princess.
Kohnstamm, M B, book-keeper H M Barry, r cor 6th and Dock.
Kolbe, C F, shoemaker M Keeler, bds same.
Kordlander, J H G, of Runge & Kordlander, r Princess, bt 4th and 5th.

L.

Lamon, W W, machinist W & W R R, r cor 6th and Walnut.
Langdon, Richard F, clerk W & W R R, r Market, bt 4th & 5th.
Langdon, Walter R, physician, Market, bt 4th and 5th, r same.
Lane, T, engineer, bds Jno Welsh.
Larkins & Hardwick, grocers, 59 Market.
Larkins, William, of Larkins & Hardwick, r cor 6th and Dock.
Larkins, P, drayman, r Princess, bt Front and Water.
Laspeyre, M, engineer W, C & R R R, bds Asa J Murray.
Latimer, Z, r cor 3d and Orange.
Laurens, H, printer Journal Office, bds Front.
Lawson, A W, mechanic A H Neff's.
Lawton, James, r cor Princess and 7th.
Leggett, John E, conductor W & W R R, r cor 6th and Walnut.
Legwin, J F, r Market, bt 3d and 4th.
Lemmerman, H, r Princess, bt 6th and 7th.
Leonard, L, clerk, S Sternberger, bds same.
Leslie, Mrs Jane, r cor Market and 8th.
Leslie, Joseph J, shoemaker, bds Mrs Jane Leslie.
Leslie, Alex, bds Mrs Jane Leslie.
Lessman, A, bakery and confectionery, S 2d, bt Market & Dock, r same.
Levy, J P, ship chandlery, &c, Dock, bt Front and Water, r Dock, bt 7th and 8th.
Levi, S, clerk S Blumenthal & Co, bds S Blumenthal.
Lewis, Mrs, boarding house, 5th, bt Princess and Chesnut.
Lewis, W M, tinner, bds 5th, bt Princess and Chesnut.

C

JAMES & BROWN,

CIVIL ENGINEERS

AND

SURVEYORS,

Office Princess Street, next to Journal Buildings,

WILMINGTON, N. C.

W. H. JAMES.   JOHN KENT BROWN.

J. R. FAULKNER.   E. M. SHOEMAKER.

RAILROAD HOTEL,

Corner Front and Red Cross Streets,

WILMINGTON, N. C.,

J. R. Faulkner & Co., Proprietors.

Choice Ale, Wines, Liquors, Cigars, &c.,

ALWAYS ON HAND.

Lewis, R James, walking man Wilmington Theatre, bds Mrs Lewis.
Lewis, T C, of Orrell & Lewis, bds Front, bt Chesnut and Mulberry.
Lippitt, Wm H, druggist and chemist, 55 Market, r 2d, bt Dock and Orange.
Lippitt, James W, clerk Wm H Lippitt, bds Mrs J J Lippitt.
Lippitt, A D, salesman Cohn & Ryttenberg, bds W H Lippitt.
Lippitt, Mrs J J, r Front, bt Orange and Ann.
Lippitt, Thos B, clerk W & W R R, bds Mrs J J Lippitt.
Lippitt, John E, merchant, r cor Front and Mulberry.
Little, C B, of Wolf, Wrouski & Co, bds cor 7th and Dock.
Little, W, printer Herald Office, bds G Prigge.
Little, V, printer Herald Office, bds J F Legwin.
Litien, Henry, clerk C Titien, bds same.
Loeb, Jacob, of J Anderson & Co, r Front, bt Dock and Orange.
London, M, attorney at law, r cor 3d and Chesnut.
London, Alex T, local reporter Dispatch Office, bds M London.
Lord, F J, Custom House, r Market, bt 2d and 3d.
Lord, Wm C, clerk Custom House, bds F J Lord.
Lord, John D, bds F J Lord.
Lord, Richard, policeman, bds P Larkins.
Lotzin, H L, watchman W & W R R, bds P Dahmer.
Love, John D, r over railroad.
Love, Edwin T, clk H McLin, r 2d bt Chesnut and Mulberry.
Love, Wm J, physician, Front bt Chesnut and Mulberry, bds A A Hartsfield.
Low, James H, r cor 5th and Market.
Lucas, E T, tinner, r cor 5th and Castle.
Lumsden, James C, saloon 21 N Front, r same.
Lumsden, Geo A, policeman, bds H H Prater.
Lumsden, H A, printer Herald office, bds Front bt Princess and Market.
Lutzen & Bloom, grocers, N Water near Red Cross.
Lutzen, R, of L & Bloom, r N Water near Red Cross.
Lynch, Thomas, grocer and commission merchant, 11 and 12 N Water.
Lynch, J J, book-keeper Thos Lynch, bds ———.
Lyon, Jacob, dry goods and clothing, 1 and 3 Market, r cor 4th and Market.
Lyons, L B, conductor W & M R R, r 6th bt Princess and Chesnut.

HARRY WEBB'S SALOON,

20 MARKET STREET,

Wilmington, N. C.

A CHOICE SELECTION OF

Ale, Wines, Liquors of all kinds, Cigars, &c. &c.

The best quality of **Pure Cognac Brandy**, for family and medicinal purposes, of our own importation, always on hand.
The table is furnished with every luxury the market can afford.
OYSTERS and other delicacies in their season.

BATE & WESCOTT,

GROCERS,

AND DEALERS IN ALL KINDS OF

Country Produce,

NO. 52, MARKET STREET,

WILMINGTON, N. C.

M.

Macomber, James, agent Adams and Southern Express Companies, r cor Market and 8th.
Macomber, Mrs R S, r cor Princess and 8th.
Maddin, James, clk A Oldham, r Market bt 6th and 7th.
Madison & Thomson, house and sign painters, Princess bt Water and Front.
Madison, L, of M & Thomson, r Front bt Market and Princess.
Magrath, John, machinist, bds James H Ellis.
Maguire, Mrs W A, r Dock bt 6th and 7th.
Mahn, W D, clk A H VanBokkelen, r 5th bt Walnut and Red Cross.
Mahoney, J R, printer Journal office, bds A J Yopp.
Mallard & King, groceries and provisions, 69 Market.
Mallard, J H, of M & King, bds L H Bowden.
Malarkey, John, S Water bt Dock and Orange.
Manning, Capt Edward W, steamer Gen Howard, (W, C & R R R passenger boat,) r cor 3d and Mulberry.
Marble, L W, engineer W & W R R, bds E Hansley.
Marcus & Kehr, dry goods, 39 Market.
Marcus, H, of M & Kehr, r 2d bt Dock and Orange.
Martin, Alfred, commission and forwarding merchant, 5 S Water, r Market bt 4th and 5th.
Martin, Eugene S, clerk A Martin, bds same.
Martin, Silas N, of Kidder & M, r 4th bt Ann & Church.
Marsteller, Geo L, of N Jacobi & Co, bds Mrs DeBebian.
Marshall, John H, pilot, r cor 2d and Red Cross.
Masonic Hall, 57½ Market, (up stairs.)
Mastin, C H, com merchant, 32 N Water, bds Mrs McCaleb.
Mason, James, mechanic Hart & Bailey's, bds ———.
Matthews, W, mechanic Hart & Bailey's, bds Princess bt Front and Water.
May, Alex, r Princess bt 6th and 7th.
McCallum, James I, r cor 4th and Orange.
McCallum, J A, clk G Z French & Co, bds 6th bt Dock and Orange.
McCaleb, Mrs M S, boarding house, Market bt 2d and 3d.
McCormick, James, manufacturer and dealer in clothing and gent's furnishing goods, 27 Market, r cor 4th and Chesnut.
McDade, W H, clk J Sherman, bds same.
McDade, W, clk Express office, bds H U Parker.

A. E. HALL,

Forwarding & Commission

MERCHANT,

NO. 22, NORTH WATER STREET,

WILMINGTON, N. C.

Personal attention given to consignments of all kinds of produce, either for sale or shipment.

W. J. BIVENS & CO.,
PROPRIETORS OF THE

ROCK SPRING SALOON,

34 North Water Street,

WILMINGTON, N. C.

A FINE SELECTION OF

ALE, WINES, CIGARS & LIQUORS,

Of all kinds, constantly on hand.

 OYSTERS in season.

McDamott, John, works Wilmington Gas Works, r Surry bt Church and Castle.
McDaniel, C S, printer Dispatch office, r cor 7th and Mulberry.
McDougald, Geo, machinist, r cor 9th and Chesnut.
McDuffie, Geo, inspector timber and lumber, r cor 4th & Red Cross.
McGowan, James, bds H M Jenkins.
McGreal, Paul, chief of city police, r City Hall.
McInnis, M, commission merchant and grocer, 16 N Water, r cor 4th and Chesnut.
McIlhenny, Thos C, r 3d bt Mulberry and Walnut.
McIlhenny, John, bds A P Repiton.
McKay, J S, mechanic W & W R R, bds L Lyons.
McKoy, T H, merchant, bds W N Peden.
McLaurin, Joseph, book-keeper Bank Cape Fear, r Market bt 8th and 9th.
McLaurin, John, book-keeper Moffit, McNeill & Co, r 2d bt Orange and Ann.
McLaurin, Hugh W, book-keeper Murray & Murchison, bds ——.
McLawlin, J D, negro teacher, bds S S Ashley.
McLeod, J C, school, 8 Front, (up stairs.)
McLin, Henry, drug store cor Market and Front, r Front bt Market and Princess.
McMillan, George D, printer Dispatch office, bds Market nr 3d.
McPherson, S W, mechanic Hart & Bailey's, bds ——.
McRae, Gen Alex, r Market bt 5th and 6th.
McRae, Col John, Pres't Bank Wilmington, and Pres't Wilmington Gas Light Company, r Mulberry bt 2d and 3d.
McRae, Alex, Jr, chief clerk John Dawson, bds mrs C K Price.
McRae, Donald, merchant, r Market bt 7th and 8th.
McRae, Walter G, store-keeper W & W R R, bds mrs C K Price.
McRae, Walter H, com merchant, 3 N Water, r cor 6th & Orange.
McRae, Rod, civil engineer, bds ——.
McRary, W H & Co, com merchants, cor Water and Princess.
McRary, W H, of W H McR & Co, r ——.
McRee, James F, Jr, physician, cor Front and Chesnut, r same.
Meares, O P, attorney at law, r ——.
Meares, Walker, r ——.
Medway, A, physician, Front bt Dock and Orange, r cor Front and Orange.
Mechanics' Hotel, Front bt Orange and Ann.
Meginney, L, Principal Wilmington Institute, cor 4th and Princess, r same.

T. S. WHITAKER,
BOOKSELLER AND STATIONER,
AND DEALER IN
MUSIC AND MUSICAL INSTRUMENTS,
ARTISTS' MATERIALS,
AND
FANCY ARTICLES
OF ALL KINDS.

No. 36, Market Street, (Sign of the Bible,)
WILMINGTON, N. C.

Wilmington Daily Dispatch,

JOHN D. BARRY, WM. H. BERNARD.

BARRY & BERNARD,

Editors and Proprietors,

Office No. 42, Market Street.

Book and Job Printing
EXECUTED ON REASONABLE TERMS,
AND IN THE HIGHEST STYLE OF THE ART.

Meier, Jos, lager beer saloon, Dock bt Front and Water, r Dock bt Front and 2d.
Merchkens, H. machinist Hart & Bailey's, r Chesnut bt 8th & 9th.
Metts, James I, salesman G Z French & Co, r ———.
Methodist Episcopal Church, (S,) cor Front and Walnut, Rev L S. Burkhead, pastor.
Methodist Episcopal Church, (S,) 5th bt Church and Castle, Rev ———, pastor.
Military Prison, cor 2d and Princess.
Mills, John, mechanic, bds J H Ellis.
Millis, John C, constable and butcher, Market House, r Dawson bt 8th and 9th.
Miller, F, shoemaker H Shutte, bds same.
Milligan, Mrs W G, r cor 2d and Mulberry.
Mitchell, B F, of Ellis & M, r 4th bt Market and Dock.
Mitchell, F H, clk Ellis & Mitchell, bds B F Mitchell.
Mitchell, James H, saloon 3 S Water, r 4th bt Market and Dock.
Mitchell, Thos Pop, clk James H Mitchell, bds same.
Moffitt, McNeill & Co, commission merchants, 4 S Water.
Moffitt, A A, of M, McNeill & Co, bds Mrs McCaleb.
Montague, W H, painter Daymon & Johnson, bds J C Daymon.
Moore, B R, attorney at law, off Journal Buildings, r N N Nixon's.
Moore, C H, grocer, 5 S 2d, r same.
Moore, M, clk C H Moore, bds same.
Moore, Roger, of Petteway & M, bds T B Smith.
Moore, Robert, baker, r Chesnut bt 4th and 5th.
Morris, Wilkes, of Cronly & M, r Front bt Church and Castle.
Morris, N, mechanic Clarendon Iron Works, bds Wilkes Morris.
Morris, Richard, accountant, r 2d bt Ann and Nun.
Morris, John C, bds R Morris.
Morris, A H, harness maker, r Chesnut bt 7th and 8th.
Morrison, George, conductor W & W R R, r Front bt Mulberry and Walnut.
Morrison, T, engineer, r cor 5th and Princess.
Morrison, R, engineer, r W G Fowler's.
Morrelle, Rev D, school, cor 4th and Cottage Lane, r same.
Mott, A, clk Dr J T Schonwald, bds ———.
Mott, David, policeman, r 9th bt Chesnut and Mulberry.
Mott, Mrs Mary, r cor 7th and Mulberry.
Mozart Hall, 17½ S Front, (up stairs.)
Munroe, J W, inspector provisions, off at Cox, Kendall & Co's, r Red Cross bt 2d and 3d.

S. BLUMENTHAL & CO.,
Corner Front and Market Sts.,
WILMINGTON, N. C.,
DEALERS IN
FANCY AND STAPLE
DRY GOODS,
BOOTS AND SHOES,
Ladies and Gent's Furnishing Goods,
AND
LADIES' AND GENT'S HATS,
OF ALL DESCRIPTIONS.

D. DRISCOLL,   J. KERRIGAN.

WILMINGTON HOUSE,
DRISCOLL & KERRIGAN,
PROPRIETORS,
Toomer's Alley, between Front & Second Streets,
WILMINGTON, N. C.,
CHOICE WINES, LIQUORS AND CIGARS.

OYSTERS,
RAW, OR COOKED IN ANY STYLE.

Munn, M, store 9th bt Mulberry and Walnut, r same.
Munson, H H, of Baldwin, M & Co, r cor 4th and Walnut.
Murray & Murchison, commission and forwarding merchants, N Water.
Murray, E, of Murray & Murchison, r Front bt Chesnut and Mulberry.
Murray, Asa J, W & W R R, r Market bt 6th and 7th.
Murray, Michael, painter, r cor Market and 7th.
Murchison, D R, of Murray & M, r ———.
Murrin, E, mechanic Hart & Bailey's, r Mulberry bt Front and Water.
Muse, J H, printer Herald office, r 2d bt Nun and Church.
Myers, George, wholesale dealer in groceries, hats, caps, boots, shoes and notions, 11 and 13 S Front.
Myers, Chas D, agent Geo Myers, r cor Market and 3d.
Myers, R C, clk Geo Myers, bds C D Myers.
Myers, Geo C, clk Geo Myers, bds C D Myers.

N.

Neff, A H, tin ware and stoves, 19 S Front, bds cor Front & Nun.
Neff, Jos H, ship chandlery and groceries cor Water and Dock, r Dock bt Front and 2d.
Neff, Geo G, clk J H Neff, bds same.
Nest, D M, mechanic Hart & Bailey's, r 6th bt Dock and Orange.
New, Solomon, clk Kahnweiler & Bro, bds cor Front and Market.
Newby, D T, clk City Hotel, bds same.
Newman, P, grocer, cor N Water and Chesnut, r same.
Newman, P, clothing, 37 N Water.
Newman, J, dry goods and clothing 14 Market, r cor 2d and Orange.
Nixon, N N, r Chesnut bt 3d and 4th.
Northrop, S & W H, steam saw and planing mills, S Water bt Castle and Queen.
Northrop, S, of S & W H N, r cor 5th and Dock.
Northrop, W H, of S & W H N, r Market bt 4th and 5th.
Northrop, James S, clk, bds W H Northrop.
Northrop, S G, engineer, r Orange bt 3d and 4th.
Northrop, Henry F, machinist, bds S G Northrop.
Nutt, John, clk Journal office, r cor 3d and Campbell.
Nutt, Henry, r cor 2d and Red Cross.
Nutt, H, baggage master W & W R R, bds Jno Nutt.

DAVID AARON,

WHOLESALE AND RETAIL DEALER IN

STAPLE AND FANCY

DRY GOODS,

READY-MADE CLOTHING,

OIL CLOTHS, CARPETING,

&c. &c. &c. &c.,

NO. 25. MARKET STREET,

WILMINGTON, N. C.

The Wilmington Herald.

DAILY & WEEKLY.

THOMAS M. COOK & CO., Editors and Proprietors.

THOMAS M. COOK,   TERRENCE V. FOLEY.

The Daily Herald

IS PRINTED EVERY MORNING, (SUNDAYS EXCEPTED.)

Terms $10 per year.............$5 for six months............$1 per month.

The Weekly Herald

IS PRINTED EVERY SATURDAY.

Terms $2 50 per year..$1 50 for six mos...$1 for three mos...50 cts per month.

The Sunday Morning Herald,

A mammoth family and literary newspaper, is printed every Sunday morning. Price ten cents per copy.

JOB WORK

NEATLY AND PROMPTLY EXECUTED.

Nunn, J F, clk, bds Mrs McCaleb.
Nye, F N, bds S W Roberts.

O.

Odd Fellow's Hall, Front, bt Market and Princess.
Ohrand, W H, grocer, Front, bt Dock and Orange, r same.
Ohrand, H, clk W H Ohrand, bds same.
Oldham, A, commission merchant and grain dealer, 6 S Water, and proprietor Cape Fear Flour Mills, cor Water and Walnut, r Front, bt Mulberry and Walnut.
Oldham, W P, salesman A Oldham, bds same.
Oldham, C W, clk Larkins & Hardwick, r ———
Orrel, J B, of O & Lewis, r 4th, bt Campbell and Hanover.
Orrel & Lewis, groceries and provisions, 8 Market.
Owen, F A, printer, Dispatch office, r cor 7th and Mulberry.

P.

Parsley, O G & Co, commission and forwarding merchants, and Importers, 6 N Water.
Parsley, O G, Sr, of O G P & Co, r Front, bt Dock and Orange.
Parsley, O G, Jr., of O G Parsley & Co, r N W cor 2d and Red Cross
Parker, H U, r cor 3d and Orange.
Patten, Wm, bakery, 44 Market, r same.
Patterson, Rev Geo, Catholic Priest, r A H NanBokkelen.
Peachman, A, harness maker B J Jacobs, r 2d bt Mulberry and Walnut.
Peck, Geo A & Co, hardware, 15 S Front.
Peck, Geo A, of Geo A P & Co, bds Capt T F Peck.
Peck, T F H, of Geo A Peck & Co, bds Capt T F Peck.
Peck, Capt T F, r 2d bt Market and Dock.
Peden, W N, proprietor Clarendon Bar, 4 Market, r 4th, bt Orange and Ann.
Penton, Wm J, seaman, r 4th, bt Nun and Church.
Penny, Henry W, clk Williams & Potter, r Front, bt Mulberry and Walnut.
Penny, W J, shoemaker J J Gay, r 5th, bt Church and Castle.
Peppinghaus, F, watchmaker, 6 S 2d, r cor 6th and Mulberry.
Perrin, Henry R, chrockery, china, glass and earthen-ware, &c, 30 Market, r 2d, bt Chesnut and Mulberry.

ATKINSON & SHEPPERSON,

Commission and Forwarding

MERCHANTS,

AND AGENTS FOR

FIRE, MARINE, AND LIFE INSURANCE COMPANIES

OF

NEW YORK AND BALTIMORE,

Office Princess Street, next to Water Street,

WILMINGTON, N. C.

WILMINGTON THEATRE,

H. M. JENKINS,   LESSEE AND MANAGER.

OPEN EVERY NIGHT.

A FULL AND TALENTED

Corps Dramatique

Is engaged for the present season of 1865-66, supported by a full

CORPS DE BALLET,

AND NUMEROUS AUXILIARIES.

An approved selection of standard **Dramas, Comedies, Tragedies, Farces, Burlettas,** &c. &c., with new **Songs and Dances,** will be presented.

No Postponement on account of weather.

Perry, James C, machinist, r Cottage Lane, bt 3d and 4th.
Perry, Mrs C D, school, Cottage Lane, bt 3d and 4th, r same.
Person & French, law office, cor S Water and Market, (up stairs.)
Person, Hon S J, of P & French, r cor 3d and Chesnut.
Peschau, Edward, merchant, cor Front and Dock, bds cor 5th and Princess.
Petteway & Moore, commission and forwarding merchants, Flanner buildings, N Water, bt Walnut and Red Cross.
Petteway, Wm H, eng'r W & W R R, r Market, bt 6th and 7th.
Petteway, James, butcher, market house, r ———
Peterson, George, printer, Herald office, bds 2d bt Church and Castle.
Peterson, Isham, clk C M Hall, r cor Front and Nun.
Philyaw, J H, r cor 4th and Princess.
Pierce, Mrs L H, r cor 2d and Chesnut.
Piggot, D, merchant, r ———
Pitts, Wm L, book keeper W B Flanner, r cor 6th and Market.
Player, T W, inspector naval stores, r 3d bt Church and Castle.
Platt, Jno T, mechanic Hart & Bailey, r Chesnut, bt 8th and 9th.
Poisson, J D., post master, r cor 5th and Mulberry.
Poisson, Jno J, clk Bradley & Woehler, bds ———
Poisson, W M, ticket ag't W & W R R, r Chesnut, bt 3d and 4th.
Polvogt, C & Co, upholsterers and paper-hangers, and dealers in furniture &c, S E cor Front and Princess.
Polvogt, Charles, of C P & Co, r Princess, bt 4th and 5th.
Polley, H N, tinner, Princess, bt Front and Water r 5th, bt Market and Princess.
Pollock, Geo W, clk post office, r Chesnut bt 3d and 4th.
Pollman, C, clk J F Heins, bds same.
Porter, Wm, provision store, cor Princess and Front, r same.
Post Office, N E cor Front and Princess, J D Poisson, P M.
Post, James F, contractor and builder, r Princess, bt 4th and 5th.
Potts, J D, telegraph operator, bds ———
Potts, S C, telegraph operator, bds ———
Powell, Mrs Sarah, r 5th, bt Mulberry and Walnut.
Praer, Frank, store Market, bt 5th and 6th avenue, r same.
Pratt, D, butcher John Bishop, bds F M James.
Prater, H, carpenter, r Market, bt 7th and 8th.
Presbyterian Church, cor 3d and Orange, Rev ——— pastor.
Presbyterian Church, Chesnut, bt 7th and 8th, Rev ——— pastor.
Price, Col Wm J, r ———
Price, A L, of Fulton & P, r 4th, bt Princess and Chesnut.

ALEX. SPRUNT,

Commission Merchant,

SOUTH WATER STREET,

Wilmington, N. C.

J. J. COX,   W. P. KENDALL, Jr.,   W. P. KENDALL, Sr.

COX, KENDALL & CO.,

WHOLESALE GROCERS

AND

COMMISSION MERCHANTS,

No. 23, North Water Street,

WILMINGTON, N. C.

Price, Mrs C K, boarding house, cor 5th and Orange.
Price, R W, clk Larkins & Hardwick, bds Mrs C K Price.
Price, W W, printer, Journal office, r cor 7th and Dock.
Price, Mrs W W, dressmaker, cor 7th and Dock.
Price, George, engineer, bds ———
Price, R A, grocer, cor Front and Queen, r same.
Prigge, G, r cor 3d and Market.
Pritchett, Geo E, clk A H VanBokkelen, bds same.
Proux, E, wagoner, r 6th, bt Chesnut and Mulberry.
Pugh, John H, bds 3d, bt Walnut and Red Cross.
Purdew, J W, mechanic A H Neff, bds 8th, bt Mulberry and Walnut.

Q.

Quince, Parker, custom house collector, r cor 6th and Dock.

R.

Radcliff, Robt S, brick mason, r Chesnut, bt 4th and 5th.
Railroad Hotel, cor Front and Red Cross, J R Faulkner & Co, proprietors.
Raleigh, T W, porter Thos Lynch, r ———
Redd, C C, r cor Market and 7th.
Reeder, H, clk E Schulken, bds same.
Repiton, Rev A P, r cor 3d and Mulberry.
Repiton, A P, Jr, r A P Repiton.
Rhodes, Hardy B, r cor Market and 10th.
Rickets, R M, clk H C Elliot, bds Princess, bt 6th and 7th.
Richardson, T W, r Water, bt Walnut and Red Cross.
Riley, James, supt Taylor's ferry, r 4th, bt Dock and Orange.
Risley, R A, r Red Cross, bt 2d and 3d.
Ritter, J W, carpenter, r 3d, bt Orange and Ann.
Roberts, T E, proprietor Clarendon Iron Works, r 5th, bt Market and Princess.
Roberts, Henry H, book keeper T E Roberts, bds same.
Roberts, S W, clk Thos Lynch, r Chesnut, bt 3d and 4th.
Robinson, Robt H, r cor Walnut and N Water.
Robinson, J S, physician, Front, bt Chesnut and Mulberry, r Orange, bt 4th and 5th.
Robinson, H H, contractor, bds J S Robinson.
Robinson, Charles H, r cor 5th and Dock.

D

JOSEPH H. NEFF,

Ship Chandler,

AND DEALER IN

Ship Stores,

GROCERIES, HARDWARE, PAINTS, OILS,

Boats, Oars, &c.,

Corner Dock and Water Sts.,

WILMINGTON, N. C.

LARKINS & HARDWICK,

WHOLESALE AND RETAIL DEALERS IN

GROCERIES, PROVISIONS,

WOOD AND WILLOW WARE,

HAVANA CIGARS, TOBACCO, LIQUORS OF ALL KINDS, &C.

No. 59, Market Street,

WILMINGTON, N. C.

W. LARKINS,   J. M. HARDWICK.

Robinson, F G, distillery, off. at Russell & Ellis, bds C H Robinson.
Robinson, Wm, printer, Herald office, r Queen, bt 5th and 6th.
Rock, Jno, policeman, r 6th, bt Nun and Church.
Rock Spring Ice House, N Water, bt Mulberry and Walnut.
Rock Spring Hotel, Chesnut, bt Front and Water, Jno Rooney, proprietor.
Rooney, John, proprietor Rock Spring Hotel.
Rose, G W, contractor and builder, r cor 6th and Mulberry.
Rosenberg, Aaron, with David Aaron, r ———.
Rosenthal, G, of A Weill & Co, r ———.
Rothwell, Mrs L P, school, 3d, bt Princess and Chesnut, r same.
Rowell, Jos W, carpenter, r 5th, bt Dock and Orange.
Rudman, A, clk N Goteberg, bds same.
Rulfs, Jno, r Red Cross, bt 4th and 5th.
Runge & Kordlander, groceries and saloon, 3 S Front.
Runge, G H W, of R & Kordlander, r 5th, bt Dock and Orange.
Rusk, C D, r 4th, bt Church and Nun.
Rush, A, r 6th, bt Castle and Queen.
Russel & Ellis, commission merchants, 10 N Water.
Russel, J B, of R & Ellis, r cor 4th and Nun.
Russel, Mrs Henry P, r cor 5th and Orange.
Russel, Yulee. clk J R Blossom & Co, bds Mrs H P Russel.
Ryan, James H, of Hedrick & Ryan, r Princess, bt Front and 2d.
Ryttenberg, J D, of Cohn & R, r ———.

S.

Samson, J & H, dry goods and clothing, 45 Market.
Samson, H, of J & H Samson, bds G Prigge.
Savage, Henry, of O G Parsley & Co, r 3d bt Dock and Orange.
Savage, Jno H, butcher Market House, r Dawson bt 7th and 8th.
Schonwald, J T, physician, Princess bt Water and Front, r cor 2d and Church.
Schulken, Henry, store cor 4th and Walnut, r same.
Schulken, E, grocer, cor Front and Mulberry, r Front bt Walnut and Red Cross.
Schulken, C, clk Runge & Kordlander, bds 3½ S Front, up stairs.
Schurback, E, clk Cohn & Ryttenberg, bds ———.
Schriver, C, store cor 4th and Harnet, r same.
Scott, O R, clk W J Bivens & Co, bds W J Bivens.
Sealey, G W, clk Harriss & Howell, r ———.
Seaman's Home, S W cor Front and Dock, G W Williams keeper.

J. T. PETTEWAY, ROGER MOORE.

PETTEWAY & MOORE,

GENERAL

COMMISSION and FORWARDING MERCHANTS,

FLANNER BUILDING,

NORTH WATER STREET,

WILMINGTON, N. C.

Prompt personal attention given to all consignments, orders, &c.

R. THORBURN,

EAGLE BAKERY,

Corner Front and Dock Streets,

(UNDER SEAMAN'S HOME,)

WILMINGTON, N. C.

A first class establishment, where can be found at all times,

Fresh Breakfast and Tea Rolls, Bread, Cakes and Pies. Also, fresh Soda and Arrow Root Crackers, and Pilot Bread.

☞ All kinds of Cakes, &c., furnished for weddings and other parties at the shortest notice.

Seaman's Bethel, Dock bt Front and Water.
Sellers, R L, constable, r 6th between Chesnut and Mulberry.
Shackelford, Haas & Co, grocers and commission merchants, 31 and 32 N Water, cor Water and Chesnut.
Shackelford, James, of S, Haas & Co, r cor Front and Chesnut.
Shaffer, O T, clk E Willis, bds Princess bt Front and Water.
Sharpsteen, W H, Verandah Saloon, 10 S Water, r Front bt Ann and Nun.
Shaw, Wm H, clk U S Q M Dept, r Red Cross bt 3d and 4th.
Shemwell, Poindexter, of Frederick & S, r City Hotel.
Sherwood, Daniel, r Princess bt Front and 2d.
Sherman, J, proprietor Globe Saloon, 1 Granite Row, Front bt Market and Dock, r same.
Shines, Mrs Eliza, r Chesnut bt 6th and 7th.
Shloss, J, clk Kahnweiler & Bro, bds S W cor Market and Front.
Sholar, Hiram, brick mason, r 5th bt Nun and Church.
Shoemaker, E M, of J R Faulkner & Co, r Railroad Hotel.
Shrank, Henry, baker A Lessman, bds same.
Shutte, Henry, boot and shoemaker, 11 N Front, r same.
Shute, Jack, painter, bds Rock Spring Hotel.
Simpson, S M, wholesale dry goods and clothing, 33 and 35 Market, and 2 and 4 N Front, N E corner, bds Miss Carrie Jones.
Sink, W M, machinist, r ———.
Singletary, F C, r Dock bt 6th and 7th.
Skipper, N, mechanic Hart & Bailey's, r Queen bt 3d and 4th.
Skull, Mrs E, r cor 5th and Walnut.
Slocum, T W, book-keeper A Oldham, bds Front bt Mulberry and Walnut.
Smaw, Frank D, Jr, bds Mrs J M Stevenson.
Smith, Wm L, cashier Bank of Wilmington, r ———.
Smith, D A, groceries, provisions, crockery, &c, 26 and 28 S Front, bds Market bt 5th and 6th.
Smith, Wm, sup't transportation W & W R R, r Mulberry bt Front and 2d.
Smith, Thos B, r cor Front and Princess.
Smith, James C, commission merchant, 2 Granite Row, Front bt Market and Dock, bds Miles Costin.
Smith & Strauss, groceries and provisions, 65 Market.
Smith, W V B, of S & Strauss, r cor 5th and Bladen.
Smith, L P, book-keeper Bradley & Woehler, bds Mrs DeBebian.
Smith, A, clk Kahnweiler & Bro, bds S W cor Front and Market.
Smith, Peter, store cor 4th and Campbell, r same.

JAMES FULTON,   A. L. PRICE.

FULTON & PRICE,
PRINTERS AND PUBLISHERS,
Journal Buildings,
PRINCESS, BETWEEN FRONT & SECOND STREETS,

WILMINGTON, N. C.

The Daily Journal,
(ESTABLISHED IN 1851.)

The oldest and most widely circulated daily paper in the State, is published six times a week, at $10 per annum, payable in advance. Daily reports of the markets, and telegraphic news, up to the hour of going to press, are given in this paper.

THE WILMINGTON JOURNAL,
(ESTABLISHED IN 1844.)

Will be resumed early in January, 1866, and issued regularly at $4 per annum, invariably in advance. This paper will contain all the principal news of the week, and all the important editorial matter of the several daily issues, together with a weekly review of the markets of the town, carefully compiled by our own reporter. This review may be relied upon as strictly correct. We also give the latest reports of the Northern and other markets.

OUR JOBBING DEPARTMENT

Is not surpassed by any establishment from Richmond to New Orleans. Having all the machinery requisite for any work required in this section of country, and being supplied with the largest and handsomest assortment of type in the State, and stationery to suit the times, we can execute promptly and in the best manner, every description of

JOB PRINTING,
SUCH AS

Cards,
  Handbills,
    Bills of Lading,
      Bills of Exchange,
        Checks,
          Bill-Heads,
Circulars,
  Pamphlets,
    Posters,
      Labels,
        Programmes, &c.

All letters on business, to insure attention, must be addressed to

FULTON & PRICE.

Sneeden, Rebecca, r Chesnut bt 8th and 9th.
Solomon, S, clk J Lyons, bds same.
Somerell, Geo M, carpenter, r cor 3d and Walnut.
Souden, E T, store Mulberry bt 8th and 9th, r same.
Southerland, J B, of Wallace & S, r 3d bt Red Cross and Walnut.
Southerland, A, boarding house Front bt Mulberry and Walnut.
Southerland, T J, of S A Currie & Co, r Princess bt 2d and 3d.
Spooner, Wm, cooper, r 2d bt Nun and Church.
Springs, Joseph, r Surry bt Church and Cast'e.
Sprunt, Alex, commission merchant, S Water bt Dock and Orange, r Princess bt 8th and 9th.
Sprunt, James, clk Worth & Daniel, bds Mrs McCaleb.
Steenken, Geo, store, cor 2d and Hanover, r same.
Stemmerman, C, store, cor 4th and Castle, r same.
Sterling, J R, r cor 6th and Chesnut.
Sternberger, J, of S, Bear & Co, r Front bt Mulberry and Walnut.
Sternberger, S, gent's furnishing goods, &c, 10 Market, up stairs.
Stevenson, Mrs J M, r Front bt Walnut and Red Cross.
Stevenson, James C, clerk O G Parsley & Co, bds Mrs J M Stevenson.
Stevenson, Daniel, bds Mrs J M Stevenson.
Stokley, James, r cor 3d and Church.
Story, S A, clk Bradley & Woehler, r 2d bt Orange and Ann.
Story, E F, clk Brown & Anderson, r 2d bt Orange and Ann.
Storer, A R, saloon, 10 Market, bds H U Parker.
Stolter & Bremer, grocers, 67 Market.
Stolter, J F, of S & Bremer, r 67 Market, up stairs.
Stolter, H, watchmaker F Peppinghaus, bds 67 Market, up stairs.
Stolter, H A, grocer, Front bt Dock and Orange, r same.
Stuart, Wm, contractor and builder, cor Front and Walnut, r cor Front and Dock, up stairs.
Strange, Robert, law office, Market bt 2d and 3d, r cor Market and 3d.
Strauss, J H, of Smith & S, r cor 4th and Hanover.
St. Thomas' Church, (Catholic,) Dock bt 2d and 3d, Rev Dr Corcoran, priest.
Styron, C W, shipping clerk Harriss & Howell, bds Mrs H P. Russell.
Sullivan, Roger R, clk James Wilson, r 5th nr railroad.
Sullivan, P, policeman, bds M Barry.
Sundheimer, J, clk Kahuweiler & Bro, r 2d bt Mulberry and Walnut.

T. J. WILLIAMS.   W. J. POTTER.

WILLIAMS & POTTER,
GROCERS,
AND
WHOLESALE AND RETAIL DEALERS IN HARDWARE,
FARMING IMPLEMENTS,

Shoes, Hats, Crockery and General Merchandise,

NO. 57 MARKET ST.,
WILMINGTON, N. C.

NORTH CAROLINA COMMISSION HOUSE.
ANDREWS & BARDIN,

OFFICE—NO. 5, SOUTH WATER STREET, (Up Stairs,)

Wilmington, N. C.

The undersigned have established a

COMMISSION AND FORWARDNIG HOUSE

In Wilmington, and offer their services for the sale of COTTON, NAVAL STORES, SHEETINGS, COTTON YARNS, TOBACCO, BACON, FLOUR, &c., &c., and to purchase for Merchants or others any goods sold in this market. Consignments and orders respectfully solicited.

We are receiving constantly from the manufacturers, small consignments of the best kind of

NORTH CAROLINA TOBACCO,

Those kinds most suitable for Country Merchants, Distillers and Turpentine Makers. We sell these lots at manufacturers' prices, and there is a clear profit to the retailer of one hundred per cent. in buying them. Orders for any number of boxes filled.

W. S. G. ANDREWS,   B. H. BARDIN,
Goldsboro', N. C.   *Brown's Wharf, Charleston.*

Sutton, Wm, blacksmith Cassidey's ship yard, r ———.
Swann, Dr John, r cor 3d and Chesnut.
Swann, F Alex, clerk, r Dr John Swann's.
Swann & Clark, carpenters, cor 3d and Princess.
Swann, Frank, of S & Clark, r Church bt 6th and 7th.
Sweeney, H, moulder Hart & Bailey's, r 2d bt Ann and Nun.
Sykes, Wm H, conductor W & M R R, r Dock bt 6th and 7th.

T.

Taylor, John A, r Market bt 4th and 5th.
Taylor, John D, bds John A Taylor.
Taylor, M P, civil engineer, bds Jno E Lippitt.
Taylor, D, clk Post Office, bds Jno Bishop.
Telegraph Office, S E cor Market and Front.
Terry, Rev R E, pastor St. John's Church, (Episcopal,) r cor 3d and Red Cross.
Thally, David, r cor 5th and Walnut.
Thomas, W G, physician, cor 4th and Market, r same.
Thompson, J W, secretary and treasurer W & W R R, r 2d bt Walnut and Red Cross.
Thompson, Mrs R M, r Market bt 5th and 6th.
Thompson, Miss Susan, r Church bt 6th and 7th.
Thomson, N, of Madison & T, r Chesnut bt 8th and 9th.
Thorburn, R, Eagle Bakery, cor Front and Dock, r 3d bt Walnut and Red Cross.
Thornton, John, r cor 5th and Harnett.
Thornton, John, Jr. bds John Thornton.
Thurston, W C, clk Kidder & Martin, r 4th bt Church and Castle.
Thurston, W J Y, clk Kidder & Martin's mill, r same.
Tierney, John C, mechanic. r Front bt Orange and Ann.
Tilley, Fletcher, r cor 4th and Red Cross.
Titien, C, store cor 3d and Orange, r same.
Toobill, D F, r 5th bt Ann and Nun.
Topham, Jas S & Co, saddlery, harness, trunks, &c, 8 S Front.
Townsend, R S. mechanic, r 3d bt Walnut and Red Cross.
Tracey, Mrs L P, dressmaker, r Cottage Lane bt 3d and 4th.
Trask, W, engineer W & W R R, r Mulberry, bt 5th and 6th.
Turner, Mrs Fannie A, transient boarding house, McRae bt Chesnut and Mulberry.
Turner, Miss Josephine, r Nun bt 2d and 3d.
Tynan, M R, salesman H M Barry, bds 2d bt Market and Dock.

A. LESSMAN,
BAKERY AND CONFECTIONERY,

No. 11, South Second St., between Market and Dock,

WILMINGTON, N. C.

A LARGE SUPPLY OF

FRESH BREAD, CAKES, CRACKERS, PILOT BREAD, FRUITS,

CONFECTIONERIES, &c.,

OF ALL KINDS, ALWAYS ON HAND.

All orders for Cakes, plain and ornamental, and baking of all kinds for weddings, parties, &c., promptly executed at the lowest rates.

S. D. ALEXANDER,

WHOLESALE DEALER IN

Brandies, Wines, Ales,

BOURBON WHISKEY, GIN, RUM, LAGER BEER,

DRAKE'S PLANTATION BITTERS,

CIGARS, &C.,

No. 10, NORTH FRONT STREET,

WILMINGTON, N. C.

A complete assortment of the best in market always on hand.

U.

Ulrich, W, of Heyer & U, r Front bt Dock and Orange.

V.

Valentine, R H C, printer Dispatch office, bds Market nr 3d.
VanAmringe, Stacey, groceries and provisions, 61 Market, r cor Front and Nun.
VanAmringe, Geo O, Sr, r cor Front and Nun.
VanAmringe, Geo O, Jr, merchant, Dock, bt Front and Water, r cor Front and Nun.
VanBokkelen, A H, commission and forwarding merchant and distiller, 40½ N Water, r Front, bt Princess and Chesnut.
VanSickle, J, tobacco, cigars, &c., 12 Market, r 2d, bt Walnut and Red Cross.
VanOrsdell, C M, photographic gallery, 40½ Market, r ———.
VanSoelen, J N, store cor 4th and Red Cross, r same.
Vick, Samuel, r cor 3d and Chesnut.
Vincent, N B, of C Polvogt & Co, r Princess, bt 4th and 5th.
Vollers, L, grocer, 3 S 2d, r cor 2d and Mulberry.
Vollers, H, of Adrian & Vollers, r cor Front and Dock.
VonGlahn, H, r cor 5th and Princess.
VonDerkammer, H, boot and shoe maker, 2d bt Mulberry and Walnut, r same.
Voss, J G, boot and shoe maker, 25 S Front, r same.

W.

Waddell, A M, attorney at law, off Market bt 2d and 3d, r 3d bt Dock and Orange.
Wade, R W, printer Dispatch office, bds cor 2d and Orange.
Waid, H, clk Express office, bds R W Blaney.
Waldron & Wilkinson, dry goods, 34 Market.
Waldron, E S, of W & Wilkinson, bds ———.
Wallace, J, baker Wm. Patten, bds same.
Wallace, S D, of Wallace & Southerland, r cor 4th and Red Cross.
Wallace & Southerland, commission merchants and agents Greensborough Mutual Insurance Co, 24 N Water, (up stairs.)
Walker, Asa K, cashier Commercial Bank of Wilmington, office cor Chesnut and N Water, (up stairs,) r cor 6th and Market.
Walker, Wm A, secretary and treasurer W & M R R, r cor 6th and Market.

DAVID C. BRADLEY, CHRISTIAN WOEHLER.

BRADLEY & WOEHLER,

WHOLESALE GROCERS,

Commission and Forwarding

MERCHANTS,

AND AGENTS

COMMERCIAL LINE STEAMERS W. P. CLYDE & FAIRBANKS,

FROM NEW YORK TO WILMINGTON.

North Water Street--West Side,

[BETWEEN CHESNUT AND MULBERRY,]

WILMINGTON, N. C.

LIBERAL CASH ADVANCES MADE ON CONSIGNMENTS.

Walker, J C, physician, Princess, bt Front and 2d, r 3d, bt Chesnut and Mulberry.
Walker, James, contractor and builder, cor Front and Walnut, r cor Front and Dock, up stairs.
Warton, R H, clerk U S Q M Department, r cor 2d and Orange.
Warren, N G, r 5th, bt Princess and Chesnut.
Ward, E R, carpenter, r cor 7th and Brunswick.
Waterbury, T, clerk H M Barry, bds ———.
Watson, Rev A A, pastor St James Church, (Episcopal,) r Market, bt 3d and 4th.
Webb, Harry, saloon 20 Market, r same.
Weill, A & Co, dry goods, shoes and clothing, 13 Market.
Weill, A, of A Weill & Co, r Market, bt 2d and 3d.
Wells, Henry, r Church, bt 4th and 5th.
Welsh, John, ship carpenter, r cor Church and 2d.
West, S M, auctioneer 6 S Water, r 3d, bt Princess and Chesnut.
West, Isham, butcher Market house, r ———.
Wescott, Ephraim, of Bate and Wescott, r ———.
Wherry, R, baker J N VanSoelen, bds same.
Whitaker, T S, books and stationery, 36 Market, r Market bt 5th and 6th.
White, Benjamin, r Market continued.
White, B F, paper hanger C Polvogt & Co, bds J W Zimmerman.
White, B F, clerk H C Elliott, bds ———.
White, P, grocer, 43 N Water, r cor 5th and Princess.
White, John, foreman Journal Office, bds Mrs S Lippincott.
White, B F, engineer W, C & R R R, bds ———.
White, P W, store cor 4th and Princess, r same.
White, John A, paper hanger C Polvogt & Co, bds W E Davis.
White, Wm L, bds J W Zimmerman.
Whitehead, James I, book-keeper, Worth & Daniel, bds Capt W B Whitehead
Whitehead, Capt W B, r Front, bt Nun and Church.
Whitman, James, r cor 8th and Market.
Whitledge, S, r Church, bt 6th and 7th.
Whitney, Mrs C C, r 5th, bt Dock and Orange.
Wilson, James, harness, saddlery, hardware, &c, 5 Market, r ———
Wilson, Wm A, book-keeper H M Barry, r cor 2d and Nun.
Wilson, James, moulder W & W R R, r 2d, bt Orange and Ann.
Wilson, Walter A, machinist W & W R R, bds W Wilson.
Wilson, W, r Red Cross, bt 3d and 4th.
Wilson, Elias R, r Guthrie's alley, bt 2d and 3d.

KIDDER & MARTIN,

AGENTS

HOME INSURANCE COMPANY,　　NEW YORK,

PŒNIX INSURANCE COMPANY,　　BROOKLYN,

MERCHANT'S INSURANCE COMP'Y,　HARTFORD.

FIRE AND MARINE RISKS AT LOWEST RATES.

Office 13 South Water Street, up stairs,

WILMINGTON, N. C.

KIDDER & MARTIN,

PROPRIETORS

COWAN

STEAM SAW AND PLANING MILLS,

WILMINGTON, N. C.

E. KIDDER,　　　　　　　　　　　　　S. N. MARTIN.

Wilson, William, merchant. bds S Witcover,
Willard, James A, commission merchant, — Water, r cor 3d and Mulberry.
Willis. Elijah, druggist and chemist, 47 Market, r cor 5th and Mulberry
Wilkinson & Co, brokers, 34 Market.
Wilkinson, J, of W & Co, r cor Market and 7th Avenue
Wilkinson, G W, of Waldron & W, bds ———.
Williams & Potter, groceries and provisions, 57 Market.
Williams, T J, of W & Potter, r Dock bt 5th and 6th.
Williams, Gertrude, r cor 2d and Craig's alley.
Williams, Thos, clk Jas H Mitchell, bds same.
Williams, George W, harbor master and keeper Seaman's Home, r same.
Williams, T D, bds T J Williams.
Williams, Jos S, bds Rev A P Repiton.
Williams, W H, salesman Kahnweiler & Bro, r 4th N of R R.
Williams & Son, W A, commission and forwarding merchants, 7 S Water.
Williams, W A, of W A W & Son, r cor 4th and Cottage Lane.
Williams, Jno F, of W A Williams & Son, bds W A Williams.
Williams, E D, printer Herald office, bds 6th bt Dock and Orange.
Wilmington Journal, Princess bt Front and 2d, Fulton & Price, proprietors.
Wilmington Dispatch, 42 Market, (up stairs,) Barry & Bernard, proprietors.
Wilmington Herald, 36 Market, (up stairs,) Thos M Cook & Co, proprietors.
Wilmington Gas Light Co, cor Castle and Surry, Col Jno McRae, president.
Wilmington Institute, cor 4th and Princess, L Meginney, principal.
Wilmington Iron and Brass Foundry, 17 S Front, Hart & Bailey, proprietors.
Wilmington House, Toomer's alley, bt Front and 2d, Driscoll & Kerrigan, proprietors.
Wilmington & Weldon Railroad, Hon R R Bridgers, president. Depot Front bt Red Cross and Campbell.
Wilmington & Manchester Railroad, O G Parsley, Sr, president. Transportation office West side N Water, bt Chesnut and Mulberry. Depot West side Cape Fear river, opp Market dock.
Wilmington, Charlotte & Rutherford Railroad, R H Cowan, president. Depot Nutt bt Bladen and Harnett.

F. W. KNOHL,
WATCHMAKER
AND
JEWELER,
NO. 9, FRONT STREET,
WILMINGTON, N. C.,

HAS ON HAND A WELL SELECTED STOCK OF

GOLD AND SILVER WATCHES,
Jewelry and Clocks,
OF ALL DESCRIPTION AND PRICES.

☞ Particular attention paid to repairing Watches, Clocks and Jewelry.

W. A. WILLIAMS,   JOHN F. WILLIAMS.

W. A. WILLIAMS & SON,
Commission & Forwarding
MERCHANTS,

Will give personal and prompt attention to the sale and shipment of COTTON, NAVAL STORES, and other produce.

Liberal advances made on consignments.

OFFICE NO. 7, SOUTH WATER STREET,
WILMINGTON, N. C.

Wilmington Theatre, Princess bt 3d and 4th, H M Jenkins, lessee and manager.
Winters, M L, clk C M Hall, bds I Peterson.
Wise, James M, bds Mrs McCaleb.
Withy, W H, mechanic A H Neff, bds ———.
Witcover, S, dry goods and clothing, 15 Market, r 2d bt Market and Princess.
Witcover, W, clk S Witcover, bds same.
Woehler, Christian, of Bradley & W, bds Mrs DeBebian.
Wolf, Wronski & Co, clothing, 40 Market.
Worth & Daniel, commission and forwarding merchants, S Water, bt Dock and Orange.
Worth, D G, of W & Daniel, r Front bt Nun and Church.
Wortheim, W, clk S Witcover, bds same.
Wood, John C, coroner, r 3d bt Nun and Church.
Wood, Robert B, Jr, clerk county court, r 3d bt Orange and Ann.
Wood, Thos F, physician, Princess bt Front and 2d, r same.
Wooster, John, r cor 3d and Dock.
Wooster, John L, bds John Wooster.
Wright, A E, physician, Market bt 2d and 3d, r cor 2d & Orange.
Wright, Wm A, president Bank of Cape Fear, r 3d bt Market and Dock.
Wright, J H, of Huff & W, r 7th bt Princess and Chesnut.
Wright, Wm E, carpenter, r 9th bt Princess and Chesnut.
Wright, Julius W, attorney at law, off Princess bt 2d and 3d, bds cor 6th and Market.
Wright, S P, of Day & W, r Market bt 2d and 3d.
Wronski, A, of Wolf, W & Co, bds cor 7th and Dock.
Wyatt, L B, tailor, r 3d bt Chesnut and Mulberry.

Y.

Yopp, W J, of Bunting & Yopp, r 5th, bt Princess and Chesnut.
Yopp, A J, r 5th, bt Chesnut and Mulberry.
Yopp, Frank, brick mason, r Chesnut, bt 8th and 9th.
Yopp, Samuel L, carpenter W & W R R, r 8th, bt Mulberry and Walnut.
Young, A D, r Market, bt 4th and 5th.
Young, Rev. —, pastor Baptist Church, r Wm Larkins.

B. F. GRADY,

Exchange Broker and Banker,

WILMINGTON, N. C.,

DEALER IN

STOCKS AND BONDS, NORTHERN EXCHANGE,

BANK NOTES, GOLD AND SILVER COIN, &C.

Collections made; Deposits Received.

☞ Office in the store of W. H. McRary & Co, at their old stand, corner of North Water and Princess Streets.

W. H. McRARY & CO.,

COMMISSION MERCHANTS,

CORNER WATER AND PRINCESS STREETS,

WILMINGTON, N. C.

Liberal cash advances made on consignments for sale or shipment.

Z.

Zekind, Alexander, clerk A Weill & Co, bds ———.
Zimmerman, J W, paper hanger D A Smith, r Market street continued.
Zoeller, E R, shoemaker H Shutte, bds same.

SHACKELFORD, HAAS & CO.,

Commission Merchants,

NO. 159 Front Street, New York,

Nos. 31 & 32 North Water St., Wilmington, N. C.

BUY AND SELL ON COMMISSION

NAVAL STORES, COTTON, LUMBER,

Cotton Yarns, &c. &c.

Constantly on hand, in Wilmington, and for sale at wholesale, a large assortment of

FAMILY GROCERIES.

SOLE AGENTS IN NORTH CAROLINA FOR THE SALE OF

WHITTEMORE'S COTTON CARDS.

REFER TO

Messrs. J. STINER & CO., 49 Vesey Street, } New York.
Messrs. MOSES & SCHIFFER, 32 Broad Street,

C. E. BURR,   A. B. BURR.

C. E. BURR & CO.,

HOUSE, SIGN,

AND

ORNAMENTAL PAINTERS,

No. 33, South Front Street,

(BETWEEN DOCK AND ORANGE,)

Wilmington, N. C.;

Keep constantly on hand a large and well selected assortment of

PAINTS, OILS, ARTISTS' MATERIALS, &c.

And are prepared to execute all orders intrusted to their care promptly and efficiently, and at the lowest rates.

SIGN AND ORNAMENTAL PAINTING

EXECUTED IN THE MOST APPROVED STYLE OF THE ART.

An efficient force of the most skillful Painters to be procured, are always engaged.

HENRY R. PERRIN,

DEALER IN

EARTHEN-WARE,

CHINA, GLASS AND STONE-WARE,

Table Cutlery,

WOOD AND WILLOW-WARE,

AND

HOUSE FURNISHING ARTICLES,

No. 30 Market Street,

WILMINGTON, N. C.

M. U. FINLAYSON, A. J. FINLAYSON.

M. U. FINLAYSON & BRO.,

COMMISSION and FORWARDING MERCHANTS,

No 5 North Water Street, (up Stairs,)

WILMINGTON, N. C.

Having established a general COMMISSION and FORWARDING HOUSE in Wilmington, we offer our services for the sale of **Cotton, Naval Stores,** and **Produce** of all descriptions, and to purchase for country merchants or others who may favor us with a call.

Consignments and orders respectfully solicited.

☞ Prompt personal attention paid to all business intrusted to our care.

JOHN DAWSON,

DEALER IN

HARDWARE, DRY GOODS,

Agricultural Implements, &c.,

(OLD STAND,)

Nos. 19 and 21 Market Street,

WILMINGTON, N. C.

P. NEWMAN,
WHOLESALE AND RETAIL

GROCER,
AND DEALER IN

WINES, BRANDIES, AND LIQUORS,

OF ALL KINDS.

WOOD AND WILLOW WARE,

FRUITS, GROCERIES, PROVISIONS,

AND

GENERAL MERCHANDIZE,

No. 33 North Water Street, (Corner Water & Chesnut,)

Wilmington, N. C.

WALTER H. McRAE,   B. H. GURGANUS.

McRAE & GURGANUS,

Commission Merchants,

WILMINGTON, N. C.,

SOLICIT CONSIGNMENTS OF

COTTON, NAVAL STORES & COUNTRY PRODUCE GENERALLY.

Prompt personal attention given to sales of produce put in our hands.

GLOBE SALOON,

J. SHERMAN, Proprietor,

NO. 1 GRANITE ROW,

WILMINGTON, N. C.

A fine selection of choice WINES, ALE, CIGARS, &c., and LIQUORS of all kinds.

Meals at all hours.

The table is always bountifully supplied with every luxury the market can furnish.

OYSTERS IN SEASON.

ELLIS & MITCHELL,

WHOLESALE AND RETAIL DEALERS IN

CORN, PEAS, OATS, RYE,

WHEAT, BRAN, HAY, FLOUR,

Meal, Hommony, &c. &c.,

No. 9 North Water Street,

WILMINGTON, N. C.

J. D. ORRELL,   T. C. LEWIS.

ORRELL & LEWIS,

WHOLESALE AND RETAIL DEALERS IN

GROCERIES, PROVISIONS, &c.,

NO. 8 MARKET STREET,

WILMINGTON, N. C.,

Keep constantly on hand every article necessary for family supplies. They have a full stock on hand and are constantly receiving fresh goods per steamers. They solicit the patronage of their friends and the public generally.

C. TIENKEN,   JOHN G. BAUMAN.

TIENKEN & BAUMAN,

WHOLESALE AND RETAIL DEALERS IN

Groceries, Provisions,

ALE, WINES, BRANDY, WHISKEY,

GIN, RUM,

AND

LIQUORS OF ALL KINDS.

CHINA, GLASS AND EARTHEN-WARE,

WOOD AND WILLOW-WARE,

Cigars, Tobacco, &c. &c.,

Nos. 20 and 22 South Front Street,

WILMINGTON, N. C.

Merchant's Exchange Hotel.

FAY & RAFFERTY, Proprietors,

NO. 51 MARKET STREET,
WILMINGTON, N. C.

There is attached to the house a first class

SALOON,

where will be kept always on hand a choice selection of the best

ALE, WINES, BRANDIES,

AND

LIQUORS OF ALL KINDS,

CIGARS, &c.

 **OYSTERS in season.**

MEALS AT ALL HOURS.

The table is always supplied with every luxury the market affords.

BILLIARD ROOMS

Open for the amusement of guests at all times.

RATES OF BOARD THE LOWEST IN THE CITY.

A. H. VANBOKKELEN,
Commission & Forwarding
MERCHANT,
41½ North Water Street,
HALL AND NUTT'S WHARVES,
(BETWEEN CHESNUT AND MULBERRY STREETS,)

WILMINGTON, N. C.

Consignments of Cotton, Naval Stores, and other Southern produce and manufactures solicited, and will fill orders for merchandize, all of which will receive his prompt personal attention.

Merchandize and other articles forwarded to any point desired.

Orders for the purchase of merchandize, and consignments of same for sale, solicited.

G. H. W. RUNGE, J. H. G. KORDLANDER.

RUNGE & KORDLANDER,
WHOLESALE AND RETAIL DEALERS IN

GROCERIES, PROVISIONS,
ALES, WINES, BRANDIES, LAGER BEER,
AND
LIQUORS OF ALL KINDS,
CIGARS, &c. &c.
MANUFACTURERS OF
SARSAPARILLA, GINGER POP, SODA WATER,
AND
BOTTLERS OF ALE & PORTER,
NO. 3 SOUTH FRONT STREET,
Wilmington, N. C.

A. ADRIAN. H. VOLLERS.

ADRIAN & VOLLERS,

WHOLESALE DEALERS IN

Groceries and Liquors,

IMPORTERS OF

HAVANA AND GERMAN CIGARS,

AND

COMMISSION MERCHANTS,

South-East Corner Front and Dock Streets,

WILMINGTON, N. C.

☞ Prompt personal attention given to the sale of

Cotton, Naval Stores,

AND

GENERAL PRODUCE.

CONSIGNMENTS RESPECTFULLY SOLICITED.

WILMINGTON BOOK BINDERY,
AND
BLANK BOOK MANUFACTORY,
JOURNAL BUILDINGS,
PRINCESS STREET,
Wilmington, N. C.

Ledgers, Journals,
AND ALL KINDS OF
BLANK BOOKS MADE TO ORDER.
ALSO,
RULING OF EVERY DESCRIPTION.

MUSIC, PERIODICALS, LAW BOOKS, &C.,

Repaired or bound in all the various styles, in the most durable manner.

☞ Old Books of every description done at the shortest notice.

P. HEINSBERGER.

CITY BUSINESS DIRECTORY,
WILMINGTON, N. C.

The following represents the principal merchants and business men in their respective branches:

AGENTS.
Insurance.

Atkinson & Shepperson, Princess near Water, Agents Fire, Marine and Life Insurance Companies of New York and Baltimore.

Dudley & Bro., 5 South Water, up stairs, Agents Underwriters' Agency, New England, (of Boston,) Globe and New York Accidental Insurance Companies of New York city.

George, E. P., office with Cronly & Morris, Agent Hartford, Atlantic, and Traveler's Accidental Insurance Companies.

Harriss & Howell, North Water, Agents North Carolina Mutual Life Insurance Company.

Kidder & Martin, corner Water and Dock, (up stairs,) Agents Home, Phœnix and Merchant's Insurance Companies.

Smith, Wm. L., office at Bank of Wilmington, Agent Phœnix Insurance Company of Hartford.

Wallace & Southerland, 24 North Water, (up stairs,) Agents Greensboro' Mutual Insurance Company.

Ocean Steamers.

Bradley & Woehler, North Water, Agents Commercial Line Steamers W. P. Clyde and Fairbanks to New York.

Barry, H M, North Water, Agent Steamers Starlight and Commander to New York.

Harriss & Howell, North Water, Agents A. C. S. S. Line Steamers Euterpe and Twilight to New York.

Sailing Packets.

Flanner, Wm. B., North Water, Agent Murray's Line to New York.
Harriss & Howell, North Water, Agents Keystone Line to Philadelphia, and New York and Boston lines.
Worth & Daniel, 20 South Water, Agents Union Line to New York and Southern Line to Philadelphia.

River Steamers.

Worth & Daniel, 20 South Water, Agents Cape Fear Line to Fayetteville.

[There are several other lines to Fayetteville, all of which come to their owners. One new line is about being established, the agent of which cannot be ascertained.]

Auctioneers.

Cronly & Morris, office No. 6 South Water, (up stairs.)
Poalk & Allen, No. 3 South Water, (up stairs.)
Shackelford, James, No. 32 North Water.
West, S. M., No 6 South Water.

Attorneys.

Baker, John A., ———.
Cutlar, DuBrutz, over Bank of Wilmington.
Empie, A., Journal Buildings, Princess bt 2d and Front.
Holmes, John L., Court House, Princess bt 2d and 3d.
London, M, ———.
Moore, B. R., Journal Buildings, Princess bt Front and 2d.
Person & French, corner Market and Water, (up stairs.)
Poisson, Fred D., Princess bt 2d and 3d, opp Court House.
Strange, R., Market bt 2d and 3d.
Waddell, A. M., Market bt 2d and 3d.
Wright, Wm. A., 3d bt Market and Dock.
Wright, Julius W., Princess bt 2d and 3d, opp Court House.

Blacksmiths

Burtt, S, Mulberry bt Front and Water.
Highsmith, Wm, 10th bt Princess and Market.

Bakers.

Thorburn, R, Eagle Bakery, cor Front and Dock.
Lessman, A, 11 South 2d, bt Market and Dock.
Patten, Wm, 44 Market.

Banks.

Bank of Cape Fear, 9 Front, bt Market and Princess.
Bank of Wilmington, 26 Front, bt Market and Princess.
Commercial Bank, cor Water and Chesnut, (up stairs.)
Savings Bank, Journal Buildings.

Billiard Saloons.

Verandah Saloon, 10 South Water.
Fay & Rafferty, Merchant's Exchange Hotel, 51 Market.

Bowling Alley.

Verandah Saloon, 10 South Water.

Bookbindery.

Heinsberger, P, Journal Buildings, Princess bt Front and 2d.

Books and Stationery.

Whitaker, T S, 36 Market.

F

Brokers, (Exchange.)

Dawson, James, 28 Market.
Grady, B F, corner Princess and Water.
Wilkinson, Jos, 34 Market.

Boots and Shoes.

Bradley, G & C, 41 Market.
French, George R & Son, 11 Market.

Butchers.

Bishop, John, Market House.
Johnson, T H & Bro, Market House.
King, Jere J, Market House.
King, John B, Market House.
Millis & Savage, Market House.
Petteway, James, Market House.

Clothing.

Aaron, David & Co, 25 Market.
Baldwin, Munson & Co, 38 Market.
Bear, Sol & Bros, 18 Market.
Bear, S & Co, 41 and 42 North Water.
Cohn & Rytenberg, 43 Market.
David, A & Co, 53 Market.
Kahnweiler & Bro, S W cor Market and Front.
Lyon, Jacob, N E cor Market and North Water.
McCormick, James, 27 Market.
Newman, P, 37 North Water.
Simpson, S M, 33 and 35 Market.
Samson, J & H, 45 Market.
Weill, A & Co, 13 Market.

Commission Merchants.

Andrews & Bardin, 5 South Water, (up stairs.)
Anderson, James & Co, 9 South Water.
Atkinson & Shepperson, Princess, near Water.
Adrian & Vollers, S E cor Front and Dock.
Bradley & Woehler, N Water, (West side,) bt Chesnut and Mulberry.
Barry, Horace M, N Water, bt Chesnut and Mulberry.
Blossom, Jos R & Co, Dock, bt Front and Water.
Chadbourn, Jas H & Co, Dock, bt Front and Water.
Cox, Kendall & Co, 23 North Water.
Eilers, H B, S E cor Market and Dock.
Finlayson, M U & Bro, 5 North Water, (up stairs.)
Flanner, Wm B, North Water, bt Princess and Chesnut.
Greene, Zeno H, 4 North Water.
Hall, A E, 22 North Water.
Harriss & Howell, North Water, bt Princess and Chesnut.
Kidder & Martin, cor Dock and Water, (up stairs.)
Keith, E A, 15½ North Water, (up stairs.)
Martin, Alfred, 5 South Water.
Murray & Murchison, North Water, bt Princess and Chesnut.
McRae & Gurganus, 3 North Water.
McRary, W H & Co, N E cor Princess and Water.
Mastin, C H, 32 North Water.
Moffitt, McNeill & Co, 4 South Water.
McInnis, M, 16 North Water.
Oldham, Alex, 6 South Water.
Parsley, O G & Co, 6 North Water.
Poalk & Allen, 3 South Water, (up stairs.)
Petteway & Moore, Flanner's building, North Water.
Russell & Ellis, 10 North Water.
Shackelford, Haas & Co, 31 and 32 North Water.
Southerland, A, South Water, bt Dock and Orange.
Sprunt, Alex, South Water, bt Dock and Orange.

VanBokkelen, A H, 41½ North Water.
Worth & Daniel, South Water, bt Dock and Orange.
Wallace & Southerland, 24 North Water, (up stairs.)
Williams, W A & Son, 7 South Water.
Willard, James A, 29 North Water.
West, S M, 6 South Water.

Cabinet Makers.

Daymon & Johnson, cor 2d and Market.
Jenkins & Bro, Princess, bt Front and Water.

Civil Engineers.

James & Brown, Princess bt Front and 2d, next West of Journal Buildings.

Crockery.

Perrin, Henry R, 30 Market.
Smith, D A, 26 and 28 South Front.
VanAmringe, S, 61 Market.

Confectioneries.

Agostini, F M, 16 Market.
Flanagan, L, 21 and 23 South Front.
Lessman, A, 11 South 2d, bt Market and Dock.

Contractors and Builders.

Post, James F, Princess bt 2d and 3d, opp Court House.
Walker, James, cor Front and Walnut.

Drugs and Chemicals.

Day & Wright, 71 Market.
Lippitt, W H, 55 Market.
McLin, Henry, N W cor Front and Market.
Willis, Elijah, 47 Market.

Dentists.

Corbin, Lillington, ———
Carr, Dr Thos B, 45½ Market, (up stairs.)

Dry Goods, &c.

Aaron, David, 25 Market.
Bear, Sol & Bros, 18 Market.
Bear, S & Co, 41 and 42 North Water.
Blumenthal, S & Co, cor Market and Front.
Bauer, F L, 23 Market.
Cohn & Ryttenberg, 43 Market.
Dawson, John, 19 and 21 Market.
Davids, A & Co, 53 Market.
Hedrick & Ryan, 5 and 7 North Front, next South of Cape Fear Bank.
Hall, C M, 29 Market.
Jacobi, N & Co, 9 Market.
Kahnweiler & Bro, S W cor Market and Front.
Lyon, Jacob, N E cor Market and North Water.
Marcus & Kehr, 39 Market.
Simpson, S M, 33 and 35 Market.
Samson, J & H, 45 Market.
Weill, A & Co, 13 Market.
Waldron, A, 34 Market.
Witcover S, 15 Market.

Express Offices.

Adams Express Company, 3 Granite Row, Jas Macomber, Agent.
Southern Express Company, 3 Granite Row, James Macomber, Agent.
City Baggage Express, J E Gadsby, proprietor, 3 Granite Row.

Furniture.

Polvogt, Chas & Co, cor Front and Princess.
Smith, D A, 26 and 28 South Front.

Grain Dealers.

Ellis & Mitchell, 9 North Water.
Oldham, Alex, cor North Water and Walnut.

Gunsmiths.

Neff, A H, 19 South Front.
Polley, H N, Princess bt Front and Water.

Groceries, &c.

Adrian & Vollers, corner Front and Dock.
Bate & Wescott, 32 Market.
Barry, Horace M, North Water bt Chesnut and Mulberry.
Bradley & Woehler, North Water bt Chesnut & Mulberry.
Bremer, H M, N E corner Front and Dock.
Cox, Kendall & Co, 23 North Water.
Egan, P & Co, 46 North Water.
Elliot, H C, 7 Market.
French, George Z & Co, 10 South Front.
Greene, Zeno H, 4 North Water.

Huggins, W T, S E corner Market and 2d.
Hussell & Bappler, corner North Water and Mulberry.
Heyer & Ulrich, 39 North Water.
Hopkins & Johnstone, 2 Granite Row.
Larkins & Hardwick, 59 Market.
Lynch, Thomas, S W corner Water and Princess.
Levy, Jonas P, Dock bt Front and Water.
McInnis, M, 16 North Water.
Myers, George, 11 and 13 South Front.
Mallard & King, 69 Market.
Neff, Joseph H, cor Water and Dock.
Newman, P, N E cor Water and Chesnut.
Orrell & Lewis, 8 Market.
Runge & Kordlander, 3 South Front.
Shackelford, Haas & Co, 31 and 32 North Water.
Smith, D A, 26 and 28 South Front.
Smith & Strauss, 65 Market.
Tienken & Bauman, 20 and 22 South Front.
VanAmringe, Stacey, 61 Market.
Williams & Potter, 57 Market.

Hotels.

Bailey's Star Hotel, 22 Front, James H Bailey, proprietor.
City Hotel, cor Market and 2d, Frederick & Shemwell, proprietors.
Farmers' House, North Water, bt Mulberry and Walnut.
Merchants' Exchange Hotel, 51 Market, Fay & Rafferty, propr'ts.
Rock Spring Hotel, Chesnut, bt Front and Water, John Rooney, proprietor.
Railroad Hotel, cor Front and Red Cross, J R Faulkner & Co, proprietors.
Mechanics' Hotel, Front, bt Orange and Ann, Thomas Daniels, proprietor.
Seaman's Home, cor Front and Dock, Geo W Williams, keeper.

Hardware.

Dawson, John, 19 and 21 Market.
Peck, Geo A & Co, 15 South Front.

Iron and Brass Foundries.

Hart & Bailey, proprietors Wilmington Iron and Copper Works, 17 Market.
Roberts, Thos E, proprietor Clarendon Iron Works, Queen, bt Surry and Water.

Ice Dealer.

Furlong, Walter, Dock, bt Front and Water.

Livery Stables.

Currie, S A & Co, cor Princess and 2d.
Steagall, R, Princess, bt 3d and 4th.

Millinery.

Bauer, F L, 25 Market.
Cohn & Ryttenberg, 43 Market,
Flanagan, L, 21 and 23 South Front.
Kahnweiler & Bro, cor Front and Market.

Merchant Tailors.

Baldwin, Munson & Co, 38 Market.
McCormick, James, 27 Market.

Manufacturers Ale, Ginger Pop, &c.

Klander, L, cor Front and Church.
Runge & Kordlander, 3 South Front.

Notaries Public.

Evans, Thomas, Dock bt Front and Water.
Loeb, Jacob, 9 South Water.
Poisson, W M, office W & W Railroad.
Smith, Wm L, office Bank of Wilmington.

Newspapers.

Wilmington Journal, Fulton & Price, proprietors, Princess bt Front and 2d.
Wilmington Dispatch, Barry & Bernard, proprietors, 42 Market, (up stairs,)
Wilmington Herald, Thomas M Cook & Co, proprietors, 86 Market, (up stairs.)
City Visitor, Kirkland & Co, proprietors.

Painters.

Burr, C E & Co. 33 South Front, bt Dock and Orange.
Fanning, P W, Front bt Orange and Ann.
Kling, Fred, 25 South Front.
Madison & Thomson, Princess bt Front and Water.

Photographic Galleries.

VanOrsdell, C M, 40½ Market.
Batchelder, W, Front bt Market and Princess.

Physicians.

Anderson, E A, Market bt 2d and 3d.
Berry, Wm A, Front bt Market and Princess.
Bradley, A O, Front bt Dock and Orange.
Cutlar, F J, over Bank of Wilmington.
Ertkenker, I F, cor Market and 2d, (up stairs.)
Freeman, Wm E, Front bt Chesnut and Mulberry.
King, J Francis, 69 Market, (up stairs.)
Langdon, Walter R, Market bt 4th and 5th.
Love, Wm J, Front bt Chesnut and Mulberry.
McRee, James F, Jr, cor Front and Chesnut.
Medway, A, Front bt Dock and Orange.
Robinson, J S, Front bt Chesnut and Mulberry.
Swann, John, corner 3d and Chesnut.
Schonwald, J T, Princess bt Front and Water.
Thomas, W G, cor Market and 4th.
Walker, Joshua C, Princess bt Front and 2d.
Wood, Thomas F, Princess bt Front and 2d.
Wright, A E, Market bt 2d and 3d.

Tobacco, Cigars, &c.

Burkhimer, Henry, 6 Market.
VanSickle, J, 12 Market.

Upholstery and Paper Hanging.

Polvogt, Chas & Co, cor Front and Princess.
Smith, D A, 26 and 28 South Front.

Watches and Jewelry.

Brown & Anderson, 37 Market.
Knohl, F W, 9 South Front.

Restaurants.

Bailey, J A, Star Saloon, Front bt Market and Princess.
Fay & Rafferty, 51 Market.
Sherman, J, Globe Saloon, 1 Granite Row.
Webb, Harry, 20 Market.

Saloons.

Bailey, J A, Star Saloon, Front bt Market and Princess.
Bivens, W J, Rock Spring Saloon, 34 North Water.
Driscoll & Kerrigan, Wilmington House, Toomer's Alley, bt Front and 2d.
Fay & Rafferty, Merchants' Exchange Hotel Saloon, 51 Market.
Faulkner, J R & Co, Railroad Hotel Saloon, cor Front and Red Cross.
Kelley, Stephen, 18 North Water.
Lumsden, James C, Half-Way House, 21 North Front, bt Princess and Chesnut.
Mitchell, James H, Gem Saloon, 8 South Water.
Meier, Jos, National Saloon, Dock bt Front and Water.
Peden, Wm N, Clarendon Bar, 4 Market.
Runge & Kordlander, 3 South Front.
Sharpsteen, W H, Verandah Saloon, 10 South Water.
Storer, A R, Wilmington Bar, 10 Market.
Sherman, J, Globe Saloon, 1 Granite Row.
Webb, Harry, Harnet Saloon, 20 Market.

Ship Chandlery.

Levy, Jonas P, Dock bt Front and Water.
Neff, Joseph H, cor Dock and Water.

Saddlery and Harness.

Jacobs, B J, 69 Market.

Topham, James S & Co, 8 South Front.
Wilson, James, 5 Market.

Steam Saw and Planing Mills.

Chadbourn, J H & Co, off Dock bt Front and Water.
Kidder & Martin, off cor Dock and Water, (up stairs.)
Northrop, S & W H, mill South Water bt Queen and Castle.

Tin Ware and Stoves.

Neff, A H, 19 South Front.
Polley, H N, Princess bt Water and Front.

Turpentine Distillers.

Blossom, Jos R & Co, Dock bt Front and Water.
Russell & Ellis, 10 North Water.
VanBokkelen, A H, 41½ North Water bt Chesnut and Mulberry.

Wines and Liquors.

Alexander, S D, 10 North Front.
Adrian & Vollers, S E cor Front and Dock.
Bremer, H M, N E cor Front and Dock.
Elliot, H C, 7 Market.
Egan, P & Co, 46 North Water.
French, George Z & Co, 10 South Front.
Hussell & Bappler, S E cor North Water and Mulberry.
Hopkins & Johnstone, 2 Granite Row.
Myers, George, 11 and 13 South Front, Chas D Myers, Agent.
Newman, P, N E cor North Water and Chesnut.
Runge & Kordlander, 3 South Front.
Tienken & Bauman, 22 and 24 South Front.

H. MARCUS,   AUGUST KEHR.

MARCUS & KEHR,

WHOLESALE AND RETAIL DEALERS IN

Fancy and Staple Dry Goods,

MILLINERY,

HATS AND CAPS, BOOTS AND SHOES,

GENT'S FURNISHING GOODS AND FANCY ARTICLES.

NO. 39 MARKET STREET,

WILMINGTON, N. C.

THOS. B. CARR, M. D.,

SURGICAL AND MECHANICAL

 ## DENTIST,

MARKET STREET,

WILMINGTON, N. C.

DENTISTS SUPPLIED WITH ARTIFICIAL TEETH

AT PHILADELPHIA PRICES.

Arrangements will soon be perfected, which will enable me to send a

SKILLFUL OPERATOR.

To my friends in the country.

PRICES OF GOLD FOR CONFEDERATE MONEY.

COMPILED BY B. F. GRADY, EXCHANGE BROKER AND BANKER, WILMINGTON, N. C.

1861.

July 15 to November 15	10 per cent.
November 15 to December 31	20 "

1862.

January 1 to February 15	25 "
February 15 to April 15	60 "
April 15 to June 1	80 "
June 1 to August 1	2 00 for one.
August 1 to October 15	2 50 "
October 15 to December 31	3 00 "

1863.

January 1 to March 1	3 00 "
March 1 to June 1	5 00 "
June 1 to July 1	7 00 "
July 1 to August 1	13 00 "
August 1 to September 1	14 00 "
September 1 to November 15	15 00 "
November 15 to December 31	20 00 "

1864.

January 1 to March 1	21 00 "
March 1 to September 15	20 00 "
September 15 to December 15	26 00 "
December 15 to December 31	50 00 "

1865.

January 1	60 00 "
January 15	65 00 "
February 1	50 00 "
February 15	45 00 "
March 1	60 00 "
March 15	60 00 "
April 1	70 00 "
April 15	100 00 "

The above are the general rates at which Confederate money sold for as compared with Gold during the time specified, or during the war.

RUSSELL & ELLIS,

Commission Merchants,

10 NORTH WATER STREET,

WILMINGTON, N. C.

PROMPT PERSONAL ATTENTION GIVEN TO THE SALE OF

COTTON, NAVAL STORES, GRAIN, &c. &c.

BALDWIN, MUNSON & CO.,

MERCHANT TAILORS,

AND DEALERS IN

CLOTHING, FURNISHING GOODS,

TRUNKS, SHIRTS, HATS, PERFUMERIES, &C.,

No. 38 Market Street,

WILMINGTON, N. C.

SOL. BEAR & BROTHERS,

18 MARKET STREET,

WILMINGTON, N. C.

MANUFACTURERS OF

CLOTHING,

AND WHOLESALE AND RETAIL DEALERS IN

Dry Goods, Hats, Caps,
BOOTS AND SHOES,
CLOTHS, CASSIMERES, FANCY ARTICLES, &C.

MURRAY & MURCHISON,

Wholesale Grocers

AND

COMMISSION MERCHANTS,

NORTH WATER STREET,

WILMINGTON, N. C.

E. MURRAY,
D. R. MURCHISON, } Wilmington, N. C. | K. M. MURCHISON,
J. T. MURRAY, } New York.

B. J. JACOBS,

MANUFACTURER AND DEALER IN

HARNESS, SADDLERY, &c. &c.

Bridles, Trunks, &c.,

MADE AND REPAIRED WITH NEATNESS AND DISPATCH.

☞ No. 69 Market Street, ☜

WILMINGTON, N. C.

S. BEAR & CO.,

DEALERS IN

STAPLE AND FANCY DRY GOODS,

Ready-made Clothing,

VALISES, CARPET BAGS, UMBRELLAS,

AND

FANCY ARTICLES,

Nos. 41 and 42 North Water Street,

Wilmington, N. C.

JOHN G. VOSS,

MAKER OF

Boots and Shoes

OF EVERY STYLE.

All orders for Work executed promptly and efficiently.

REPAIRING

DONE NEATLY AND WITH DISPATCH, AND AT THE LOWEST RATES.

No. 25 South Front Street,
WILMINGTON, N. C.,

POALK & ALLEN,
SHIPPING and COMMISSION MERCHANTS,

No. 3 South Water Street,
WILMINGTON, N. C.

REFER TO

HARRISS & HOWELL,	WM. M. HARRISS,	WM. B. FLANNER,
	J. SHACKELFORD.	

☞ We also sell at AUCTION under license of J. Shackelford, who is concerned with us in this line of our business.

HENRY SHUTTE,

MANUFACTURER OF

BOOTS AND SHOES,

KEEPS ALWAYS ON HAND A GENERAL ASSORTMENT OF

SHOE STOCK,

NO. 11 NORTH FRONT STREET,

WILMINGTON, N. C.

KELLY'S SALOON,

NO. 18 NORTH WATER STREET,

WILMINGTON, N. C.

Keeps constantly on hand a large and choice selection of fine

IMPORTED AND DOMESTIC LIQUORS

OF ALL KINDS.

OYSTERS in their season.

HAVANA CIGARS, &c.

STEPHEN KELLY, Proprietor.

GENERAL DIRECTORY.

MUNICIPAL GOVERNMENT.

Mayor,
JOHN DAWSON.

Commissioners.

James Shackelford ....Alfred Martin.
John G. Bauman. ....Stephen D. Wallace.
Eli Murray......... ....Wm. S. Anderson.

Mayor's Court meets at 3 o'clock, P. M.

City Clerk and Treasurer,........................... T. W. Anderson.
City Tax Collector. .... Thomas H. Howey.
City Surveyor. .... Wm. H. James.

City Police.

Chief of Police, ... Paul McGreal.
Assistant Chief of Police, ... John Griffith.
Chief of Night Police,........................... L. W. Hannon.

Fire Department.

Chief Engineer, ... James Mitchell.
Assistant Chief Engineer,....................... James Macomber.

FIRE WARDENS.

Chief Fire Warden,............................ W. Burkhimer.

Assistant Fire Warden,..............................A. H. VanBokkelen.
Avon E. Hall,..James H. Ryan.
James McCormick.......................................James G. Green.
              E. Schulken.

Howard Fire Company.

President, ...R. Bate.
Treasurer, ...G. H. W. Runge.
Secretary,..H. Vollers.
Foreman,...J. Spelman.
1st Assistant F   T. Bremer.
2

C
S
E

RAIL ROADS.

Wilmington and Weldon Rail Road.

President,...R. R. Bridgers.

DIRECTORS.

P. K. Dickinson..W. A. Wright.
S. D. Wallace..Alfred Martin.
A. H. VanBokkelen. ....Eli Murray.
Edward Kidder...John Everett.
W. D. Faircloth...John Norfleet.

OFFICERS.

Engineer and Superintendent............ ....S. L. Fremont.
Secretary and Treasurer,...................... J. W. Thompson.
Superintendent of Transportation,............William Smith.
General Ticket Agent and Clerk,............Wm. M. Poisson.
General Freight Agent, ...G. L. Dudley.
Master Mechanic, ...John F. Divine.

SCHEDULE OF PASSENGER TRAINS.

Leave Wilmington daily at.................................4.00 P. M.,
Arrive at Weldon daily at................................8.00 A. M.,
Leave Weldon daily at....................................2.00 P. M.,
Arrive at Wilmington daily at............................5.40 A. M.

Connects at Wilmington with Wilmington & Manchester Railroad; at Goldsboro' with North Carolina Railroad, and Atlantic & N. C. Railroad; at Weldon with trains to and from Petersburg by Gaston Ferry, and on direct to Norfolk and Washington.

Wilmington and Manchester Rail Road.

President,..Oscar G. Parsley, Sr.

DIRECTORS.

John Dawson...................................Henry Nutt.
John A. Taylor...............................N. N. Nixon.
James G. Burr,..............................Richard Bradley.
J. Eli Gregg................................— — Moore.
　　　　　　　Maj. — — Haynesworth.

OFFICERS.

General Superintendent,...................Henry M. Dran..
Assistant Superintendent, ...W. H. McDowell.
Secretary and Treasurer, ...William A. Walker.
General Freight Agent,....................John L. Cantwell.

SCHEDULE OF PASSENGER TRAINS.

Leave Wilmington daily at....................6:00 A. M.,
Arrive at Florence at ....6.30 P. M.,
Arrive at Kingsville at....................1.25 A. M.,
Leave Kingsville dai'y at....................7.35 P. M.,
Arrive at Florence at....................2.05 A. M.,
Arrive at Wilmington at....................3.05 P. M.

TABLE OF DISTANCES FROM WILMINGTON TO

Flemington,	34 miles.	Florence,	107	miles.
Whiteville,	44 "	Timmonsville,	119	"
Fair Bluff,	63 "	Lynchburg,	127	"
Nichols',	72 "	Mayesville,	137	"
Mullins',	78 "	Sumter,	146	"
Marion,	86 "	Manchester,	157	"
Pee Dee,	94 "	Kingsville,	171	"
Mar's Bluff,	101 "			

Connects at Florence with North Eastern Railroad, and Cheraw and Darlington Railroad ; at Kingsville with South Carolina Rail Road.

Wilmington, Charlotte and Rutherford Rail-Road.

President,....................Robert H. Cowan.

DIRECTORS.

Samuel J. Person ....Joseph Green.
John A. McDowell....................Robert S. French.
Walter L. Steele....................Stephen W. Cole.
Samuel H. Walkup....................E. Nye Hutchinson.
Haywood W. Guion....................C. C. Henderson.
A. G. Logan.

OFFICERS.

Superintendent,........................Roger P. Atkinson.
Treasurer and Master of Transportation....W. H. Allen.
Master Mechanic,........................J. B. Gayle.
Freight Agent............................I. T. Alderman.

SCHEDULE.

Leave Wilmington every Tuesday, Thursday & Sat'day, at 8 A. M.
Arrive at Sand Hill on same days at......................4 P. M.
Leave Sand Hill every Monday, Wed'sday & Friday, at..7 A. M.
Arrive at Wilmington on same days at....................3 P. M.

TABLE OF DISTANCES FROM WILMINGTON TO

Riverside,	5	miles.	Moss Neck,	76	miles.
North West,	15	"	Red Banks,	84	"
Marlville,	26	"	Shoe Heel,	89	"
Rosindale,	38	"	Laurinburg,	95	"
Brown Marsh,	46	"	Laurel Hill,	101	"
Bladenboro',	54	"	Sand Hill,	110	"
Lumberton,	68	"			

BANKS.

Bank of Cape Fear,

No. 9 North Front street, between Market and Princess.
President—Wm. A. Wright.
Cashier—James G. Burr.
Book Keeper—Jos. McLaurin.

DIRECTORS.

P. K. Dickinson........................John Wooster.
James Anderson........................Robert Strange.
Daniel L. Russell......................Wm. B. Giles.
Jesse H. Lindsay......................Adam Empie.
George R. French......................Sion H. Rogers.

Bank of Wilmington,

Front street, between Market and Princess
President—John McRae.
Cashier—William L. Smith.

DIRECTORS.

John McRae	Alfred Martin.
Stephen D. Wallace	William H. McRary.
William A. Berry	George R. French.

Levi A. Hart.

Wilmington Savings Bank,

Journal Buildings, Princess street, between Front and 2d.
President—John A. Taylor.
Cashier—P. W. Fanning.

DIRECTORS.

John A. Taylor	Alfred Martin.
Stephen D. Wallace	Daniel Fergus.

Alfred Alderman.

Board of Directors meet Tuesday of each week.

Commercial Bank of Wilmington,

Office corner Chesnut and North Water streets, (up stairs.)
President—Oscar G. Parsley, Sr.
Cashier—Asa K. Walker.

DIRECTORS.

Oscar G. Parsley	Eli Murray.
Henry Nutt	John D. Bellamy.
N. N. Nixon	W. G. Thomas.
Bennet Flanner	Z. Latimer.

Edward Kidder.

Churches.

Baptist, cor Orange and 6th, Rev. ———, pastor.
Baptist, Front, bt Ann and Nun.
Baptist, (now building,) cor Market and 5th, Rev. Mr. Young, pastor. (Services held at City Hall.)
Episcopal, (St. James,) cor Market and 3d, Rev. A. A. Watson, pastor.
Episcopal, (St. John's,) cor 3d and Red Cross, Rev. R. E. Terry, pastor.
Episcopal, (St Paul's,) cor 4th and Orange, Rev Geo Patterson, pastor.
Lutheran, (now building,) cor Market and 6th.
Methodist Episcopal, cor Front and Walnut, Rev L S Burkhead, pastor.
Methodist Episcopal, (S,) 5th, bt Nun and Church.
Presbyterian, (1st,) cor 3d and Orange.
Presbyterian, Chesnut, bt 7th and 8th, Rev. ———, pastor.
Roman Catholic, (St Thomas,) **Dock**, bt 2d and 3d, Rev Dr Corcoran, priest.
Seaman's Bethel, Dock, bt Front and South Water, Rev ———, pastor.

Oakdale Cemetery.

President,..Edward Kidder.
Secretary and Treasurer,.......................P. W. Fanning.
Superintendent,....................................Timothy Donlon.

DIRECTORS.

William A. Wright............................John A. Taylor.
Stephen D. Wallace..........................George R. French.
Edward Kidder.

Port Government.

COMMISSIONERS OF NAVIGATION.

P. W. Fanning, Chairman.

A. P. Repiton..B. F. Mitchell.
John A. Taylor.......................................James Anderson.
Clerk and Treasurer,............................Thos. H Howey.
Harbor Master,....................................G. W. Williams.
Port Physician,.....................................Dr. J. C. Walker.

PORT WARDENS.

Charles D. Ellis....................................George Harriss.

Silas N. Martin.

EXAMINING COMMITTEE.

Charles D. Ellis...................................A. Guthrie.

J. S Price.

Seaman's Friend Society.

(CONSTITUTED FEB. 4TH, 1853.)

President—Charles D. Ellis.
Secretary and Treasurer—B. F. Mitchell.

EXECUTIVE BOARD.

John McRae,..T. C. Worth.
Oscar G. Parsley, Sr............................Charles D. Ellis.

TRUSTEES.

Oscar G. Parsley, Sr............................Henry Nutt.
John McRae..Charles D. Ellis.
William A. Wright...............................Armand J. DeRosset.
George R. French.................................George Harriss.
P. K. Dickinson....................................B. F. Mitchell.

Joseph H. Flanner.

Keeper of Seaman's Home,................George W. Williams.

Seaman's Home, cor Front and Dock streets.

SECRET SOCIETIES.

Concord Chapter No 1—Masonic.

Alfred Martin, ...High Priest.
Thomas B. Carr,..................................King.
P. W. Fanning,..Scribe.
Thomas M. Gardner,..................................Captain of the Host.
A. J. Howell,....................................Principal Sojourner.
Asa A. Hartsfield,.................................... Royal Arch Captain.
Jacob Lyons,..Treasurer.
A. Paul Repiton,....................................Secretary.

Meets on the first Monday of every month, at Masonic Hall.

St. John's Lodge No. 1—Masonic.

Thomas M. Gardner,..................................Master.
Ed. Wilson Manning, ...Senior Warden.
Joseph B. Russell, ...Junior Warden.
Richard J. Jones,....................................Treasurer.
Wm. M. Poisson, ...Secretary.
Horace A. Bagg,.................................... Senior Deacon.
James O. Bowden,..................................Junior Deacon.
Henry C. Hewett,..................................Tyler.

Meets on the last Monday in every month, at Masonic Hall, 57½ Market, (up stairs.)

Cape Fear Lodge No. 2—I. O. O. F.

John J. Conoley, N. G .... R. J. Jones, V. G.
Wm. L. Smith, Secretary........... Thomas H. Howey, Treasurer.

Meets at Odd Fellows' Hall, cor Front street and Toomer's alley, (up stairs,) Tuesday evening of each week.

Public Halls.

City Hall, cor Princess and 3d.
Wilmington Theatre, Princess, bt 3d and 4th, H M Jenkins, Lessee and Manager.
Mozart Hall, 19½ South Front, (up stairs,) Jas H Bailey, Lessee.

County Government.

Sheriff, ...Samuel R Bunting.
Register of Deeds, &c,............................Geo W Pollock.

CONSTABLES.

R L Sellers, Elkanah Allen, and John C Millis.

Courts.

SUPERIOR COURT.

Clerk, ...Horace A Bagg.

COUNTY COURT.

Chairman, ...James Shackelford.
Clerk,..Rob't B Wood, Jr.

COURT OF EQUITY.

Clerk and Master, ... Fred D Poisson.

MAGISTRATE'S COURT.

Special Magistrate,.............................. John J Conoley.
Meets 10 o'clock A M, daily, (Sundays excepted.)

Inspectors.

PROVISIONS AND COTTON.

D E Bunting, Wm J Yopp, John W Monroe.

NAVAL STORES.

John C Bowden, James O Bowden, Alfred Alderman, Archibald Alderman, John S James, Thos W Player.

TIMBER AND LUMBER.

L H Bowden, James Alderman, George McDuffie.

WOOD.

Franklin V. B. Yopp, John Potter.

Schools.

Wilmington Institute, cor 4th & Princess, L. Meginney, principal.
Wilmington Male and Female Seminary, cor 2d and Chesnut, Geo W Jewett, principal.
J C McLeod, cor 5th and Princess.

Wilmington Gas Light Company.

President—Col John McRae.
Secretary and Treasurer—John J Conoley.
Superintendent—James Darby.

DIRECTORS.

Z Latimer.	E Kidder.	W G Thomas.
Geo R French.	Stephen D Wallace.	A J DeRosset.

United States Officers.

CUSTOM HOUSE.

Collector—Parker Quince.   *Deputy Collector*—Fred J Lord.
Surveyor—F A Fuller.

Inspectors.
Thos M Gardner.   Henry D Gilbert.   Wm F Burch.

POST OFFICE.

J D Poisson, *Postmaster*.
George W Pollock, D Taylor, *Assistants*.
Office open from 9 A M to 5½ P M : Sundays 9 A M to 10 A M. Northern and Eastern Mail closes at 3 P M : Southern Mail closes at 5½ P M : W, C & R R R closes at 6 P M.

MILITARY.

Maj Gen Geo Crook, commanding district, headquarters 2d, bt Market and Princess.
Col N Goff, Jr, commanding post, headquarters Front, bt Princess and Chesnut.
Capt H B Blackman, depot and post quartermaster, office Post Office building, cor Front and Princess.
Capt E Jones, commissary, office Post Office building.
Lieut J Lukens, ordnance officer, office Post Office building

FREEDMAN'S BUREAU.

Maj C J Wickersham, superintendent district, headquarters cor Front and Chesnut.
Maj J C Mann, financial agent, headquarters cor Front and Chesnut.
Lieut R A Draker, superintendent sub district, headquarters opp Court House.
Dr E Wynants, surgeon.

APPENDIX.

Owing to unavoidable circumstances, the following names were omitted, with the exception of those marked thus *, who have made changes in their places of business or residence:

Alexander, S D, wines and liquors, 10 North Front.
Bradley, G & C, boots and shoes, 41 Market.
Bachelder, Wm, picture gallery, Front, bt Market and Princess.
*Cazaux, A D, bds Mrs H P Russell.
Cassidey, Henry C, bds James Cassidey.
Finlayson, M U & Bro, commission merchants, 5 South Water, (up stairs.)
Gilbert, C F, jeweller F W Knohl, bds Bailey's Hotel.
Gurganus, B H, of McRae & Gurganus, r Col John McRae.
*Hall, Edward D, r Orange, bt 2d and 3d.
Hill, Fred C, r W A Wright.
*Keith, E A, commission merchant, 15 North Water.
Klein, John C, butcher Washington Market, 58 Market.
Klein, David, r cor Mulberry and 10th.
*McRae & Gurganus, commission merchants, 3 North Water.
McLauchlin, B L, clerk Day & Wright.
McLauchlin, J L, baggage master W & M R R.
McAlister, W, at James & Brown.
Strauss, John W, grocer 2d, bt Hanover and Brunswick, r same.
Strauss, Wm H, store cor 4th and Hanover, bds John W Strauss.
Sullivan, Uriah, wood dealer, r Chesnut, bt Front and Water.
Vonglahn, C, r 2d, bt Hanover and Brunswick.
Zoehler, Charles, painter Fred Kling, r H Bremer.

www.ingramcontent.com/pod-product-compliance
Lightning Source LLC
Chambersburg PA
CBHW021918180426
43199CB00032B/526